WHY I WEAR CLOTHES TO BED

AND OTHER TALES FROM THE INN

B. B. BROWN

DEDICATION

I owe my son, Todd, so much. He has more courage and fortitude than anyone I know and was a great inspiration to me when he wrote and had published a well-written book about a very tough topic. He received thank yous from all over the country and abroad for writing this book. Many readers wrote to him and claimed he had saved their lives or had made them proud of whom they had become. One young man said the book gave him the courage to follow his dream. He ended up in the Big Apple in the same work environment as Todd's sister. One day this man was telling Tammy all about Todd's book. She proudly said, "The author of that book is my brother." Todd's talent gave me the incentive to tackle my own project, my inn memoir, before I forgot the people and topics I wanted to mention and honor. Thank you Todd. I love you very much.

CONTENTS

ACKNOWLEDGMENTS

Without my guests there would be no stories from the inn. This business brings people together from far and near. There are many that come often and are so much fun to know. On the far other side there are the characters that cause the problems and make life miserable for me the few days they are here. After they leave their names get noted on my May Not Return List. I am very glad to see them go but realize a few days later that my life would be much more boring had they not come.

In nearly 30 years in business, I have never had any major damage, bad checks, or items stolen. There are a certain percentage of people in our society that are insensitive to others and perhaps even convicts at one time or other. I am lucky to have met up with very few.

I have books in all my rooms and they seem to be appreciated by many. They are read and left where they are found. Books that guests have brought and read while here are often left on the shelves along with mine. The number of books just keeps increasing.

Guests often ask me out to dinner, invite me to stay at their homes when I am traveling near them, or leave gifts for me. It is interesting to talk with people I have met from Maine to Australia and beyond. I have learned so much from so many of them. I am thankful for my family, my friends, and my business. I am also very thankful to so many nice people that came to the inn as guests and became friends. All my guests have added entertainment through the years and made my life fun and interesting.

SEACROFT INN

HOW IT ALL BEGAN

MAKING THE DECISION AND DEVISING A PLAN

DAVE AND THE PRONOUN WE

LOCATION, LOCATION, LOCATION

A NON-TRADITIONAL B&B

MAKING THE DECISION AND DEVISING A PLAN

It was the best of times. It could have been the worst of times. We were at the Crossroads of our lives. At 50 years old and with three kids all in college at the same time we were edging toward that inevitable empty nest. Our youngest was just entering Northeastern, our middle child was a junior at NYU, and our oldest was graduating from UConn. We were very proud of all of them for their many accomplishments. They were all in a happy place in their lives, but we were racking up a huge debt in college bills. Our goal was for them to graduate debt free but we in turn were not.

We were living on a lovely horse farm in a small Maine town. My husband Dave was commuting long distance to the University of Maine where he was a professor in education after retiring from the superintendency in the school district where we lived. He was a wonderful educator, loving to teach what he knew threaded with a good deal of common sense, relating to all kinds of students who loved him and learned from him. But, working in education does not make one rich and does not pay all the college bills.

Dave did a lot of thinking on his long commutes and came home one night all excited. He said, "Let's move back to Bar Harbor where we can find a business to augment my paycheck from the University." We had lived there for three years in the early 60's and loved the town and Acadia National Park. Two of our children were born there and we had established shallow roots. We had moved away to improve Dave's educational career but often returned to hike, bike, x-c ski, kayak, and of course visit old friends. We often talked about returning to live there someday. It always felt like our special place.

It was the same distance for Dave to commute to work that he was already doing from our farm. We talked about possibly finding a combined home and business. We knew we were willing to do about anything as long as it was legal and didn't have anything to do with food. Restaurants were out. But other than that we were open to any suggestions and had confidence that we could do whatever it took.

We lined up a realtor who could show us what was available. She seemed stuck on the B&B business so why not take a look. The first place we checked was an 1890 Victorian on Albert Meadow with an ocean view. Although it was right near the Shore Path in town we had never walked down this street. The building needed some fixing up but we shared a look and a smile knowing without any words that we had agreed – this was it. It was a waste of time to look further.

The 6000 square foot building was divided into three apartments, but the realtor kept saying it could be a B&B. Dave looked very serious and told her that we had been married for over 30 years and I had never cooked him breakfast – and besides that I am not at all sociable in the morning. But we knew it could work and we would figure it out. Maybe I could be sociable mornings but the food thing was still an issue.

WHY I WEAR CLOTHES TO BED

We were not risk takers and couldn't really afford it but we had the farm for collateral and a generous mother with a down payment loan. We just felt it was something we wanted to do and we would do what we had to to make it successful. We couldn't close until the owner got rid of the tenants who had contracts, but we ended up moving into the main apartment with all our belongings and two dogs and rented it for six months. This gave us just enough time during the winter to close the sale and create rooms with private baths out of the other two apartments.

We talked about creating something that we would like. We had never stayed in a B&B preferring budget motels. We liked a very clean space with a kitchenette in a great location. Location was our biggest asset. Most of our rooms have their own entrances offering the privacy of a motel but the décor and comfort of home.

So without me preparing any kind of food, our B minus a B was born. We called it Seacroft, a name from its past, which to me sounds as if it should be a home by the sea with a rocky foundation. It fit just right. We officially opened in June, 1991. Since we are located on a tiny dead end street with low visibility for tourists looking for a room, we called all our acquaintances and friends who owned lodging facilities as well as the very helpful Chamber of Commerce. Guests started to come and they spread the word giving us a very good first season.

Dave was working Monday through Friday at the University and that left me to tend the inn. I loved meeting people and doing the physical work. The physical work was time consuming, cleaning and laundering all the sheets and towels for fifteen guests. The washers and dryers were in the basement that meant I went up and down the narrow spiral staircase many times a day. The laundry baskets I had were too large to clear the railings so I had to buy smaller ones. I also thought I should hang the sheets outside just like my mother had all those years. They smelled so fresh and special.

It was also the time before the internet and the phone rang and rang. Since I was alone I had to stop what I was doing and answer the same questions over and over as well as take reservations. We soon found out we needed to get a deposit and establish a cancellation policy or folks would often cancel the last minute. So much for being too idealistic and trusting the public to do the right thing.

Dave mowed the lawn and cleaned bathrooms on the weekend. Guests loved his down home personality and the jokes he told in his thick Maine accent. I found little bits of time here and there to spend with guests, answering their questions, helping them plan their day, and getting to know a little bit about them.

When we had traveled we did not care for room service and always turned it down preferring to find the room the way we had left it. We soon offered our guests discounts if they chose to forego the daily housecleaning. This was very popular as most people are always willing to save money. It was popular with us also as it was time consuming to get into every room every day. Many times we did not know when guests were in since they often walked everywhere because of our in town location. Their cars were parked in their spots but more times than not they were not still in their rooms. We would wait around all morning for them to leave and then we would see them walking back into the driveway.

We soon offered coffee and tea and shortly after a continental breakfast basket. Since we had the small kitchenettes and we are right in town with many restaurants within walking distance we offered an additional discount for no breakfast. That worked well, but we later found out if we charged an extra fee for housekeeping and breakfast instead of offering discounts it worked even better. So nearly 30 years later we are still doing that. I can often go weeks without making a blueberry muffin and that is just fine with me. I found out that people do like options and like the fact that they could get breakfast at Seacroft but more times than not most prefer to fix their own or dine out.

People often refer to us as a B&B and I quickly tell them we are an inn, Seacroft Inn. I am not sure why I dislike to deal with breakfast so much but all my repeat guests know this and know better than to order the breakfast basket. They also started coming to the inn before we offered breakfast and had gotten used to doing their own thing.

There are a lot of people who have stayed at our inn and I must say I like so many of them. I consider some of them good friends and feel guilty when I charge them the going rate. They often offer me a room in their homes if I am passing through their towns. Needless to say I have never taken them up on their generous offers. There are a lot of stories I would like to share about these friends and how they have made my business so much fun and successful.

There are also some interesting characters who have only come once since they made my list of Those Who May Not Return. Our population has a certain percentage of those with mental illnesses, alcohol problems, or who are just plain bad actors. But I must say they make my life as an inn owner more interesting. And they will indeed be part of my tales from the inn.

My customers represent a large part of my story and I will get to them later. But first I will describe a few more things about the inn and how it became the place it is today.

DAVE AND THE PRONOUN WE

The two of us ran the inn for the first 18 years. Dave liked the business and was proud of what we had created but he didn't love it like I do. Before he got ill he said that if something happened to me he would sell the inn since he had rather just stay in education, his first love. He also said he knew if something happened to him that I would keep it and run it myself. He realized that even though he was a huge help in many ways, I was the driving force to stay on top of things and I loved the business experience.

Dave was a fighter and loved life but the big C is an evil manipulator and won the war. I lost my partner for life, my best friend for nearly fifty years, and where Seacroft was concerned, my business partner. He could handle the big things and I could tolerate the small insignificant things. When something popped up that needed fixing we automatically knew whose job it would be to fix it.

We would plan and implement improvements together. We would make up funny stories about our guests while cleaning rooms. You can tell a lot about people when you clean up after them. When we first opened we learned that most people shed hair – lots of hair. There were hairs everywhere. I had to change blankets because our less expensive ones would suck in every loose hair and it would become permanently embedded. I had to purchase washing machines with better filters. Dave said when we got rich we would restrict our guests to the bald ones.

I usually use the pronoun WE since Dave and I created the business and we did all the work inside and out. Dave insisted that we keep it simple. He wanted me to be able to pretty well run it by myself since he was tied up at the University. I might have tried to expand it since we had the space to add a couple more rooms. We ended up with six rooms, and a two-bedroom unit for paying guests. After losing Dave, I still often use the pronoun WE since my grown kids are very supportive. They help when visiting whether cleaning, planting, doing computer work, or making suggestions.

But they all have their own careers and live far away. I knew I couldn't do everything by myself so I looked around for some cleaning help for ten hours a week. Getting used to dealing with employees was not pleasant. It was hard to find someone for the short hours and my first helpers obviously needed extra jobs. They would often have to leave before getting their work done. I had two girls who came as a pair. Big mistake. They thought that ten hours meant ten hours each. They were always chatting and for some reason they couldn't chat and work at the same time. Whenever I asked them to do something there was the inevitable eye roll or sigh. I would often carry the heavy laundry for them since they seemed to struggle with it. I had extra expenses with Workman's Comp that I had never had before. All this was taking the fun out of running the inn and I was exhausted.

I got through the first year and luckily Kady showed up that fall asking for a job for the next season. She had been a guest for years so I knew her well. She was turning fifty and wanted to quit her job in another state and spend her summers in Bar Harbor. She could be flexible about what she did. I offered her twenty hours a week and found her a place to live. She moved into an inn right next door and became the night person there for a free place to stay. She also became an innkeeper there a couple of evenings a week. With a third job as innkeeper in yet another inn she worked fifty hours a week.

Kady was not then and still is not afraid of work. She always puts me first giving me the hours and time I need and is willing to do anything that needs to get done (that is except cutting up a pineapple, but that is another story). It has been eight seasons now. I am lucky to have found her. She now wants more hours and I want less so she just takes over a good deal of time. So with the help of my kids and Kady and with Dave very much still in my heart I am still using the pronoun WE.

LOCATION, LOCATION, LOCATION

Now where have we heard that before? The saying has been used many times and I presently have it on my Website. Location is a starting point for any business. The old cliché, "You can't expect to sell ice to Eskimos," but it might be a great business in Fiji. You can't expect to have a successful lodging business if tourists have no reason to come to you.

When Dave and I drove down Albert Meadow for the first time we were enchanted. We had lived in this town right out of college for three years and had never been down this street. There at the end was the ocean glistening in the sunshine. There was very little traffic, only a few houses, and the street was very quiet. Just three houses up from the ocean was the property we were going to size up for a future home and business.

It was a white Victorian with shutters and decks with ocean views. Our realtor said it could no doubt be permitted as a B&B. At the time it had three apartments but after checking them out we knew that this could be a great home for us and we could make it into a comfortable seven room inn with very little construction.

Our motto is By the Shops, By the Shore and that

describes a premium location. We felt guests would love the location since they could walk down a quiet street about two hundred yards and be right on the water. The Historic Shore Path is there where one may meander in either direction with gorgeous homes on one side and the ever changing ocean on the other.

This path is unique as it has always been on private property and is available for public use because of the owners' generosity. I personally love to walk along the shore every morning when I can. The views are always different with fog patterns, sunrises, wildlife, tides, and boats of all kinds. Sometimes the water is like a mirror reflecting the sun and sometimes there are huge waves breaking up over the Porcupines. My guests can grab a cup of coffee and sit on a rock to view this majestic wonder or they can stroll on like I do.

I always mention to new guests that they must try going to the left when they leave the driveway. I once discovered that one couple always went to the right to the shops and pubs thinking that is what Bar Harbor is all about. It is true that a short walk gets one to over fifty eateries and as many shops all within a half mile. When that couple took a left turn instead of their usual route as I suggested, they were delighted to have found it before they departed the next day.

The serenity is to the left; the circus is to the right. It all depends on what you are looking for. The ocean is magnificent and the town in lively and fun. There are beautiful parks with antique fountains and gorgeous gardens. There is live music around every turn. For years the town band has played twice a week in season just up the street. Eighty locals from eight to eighty crowd into the gazebo and play an assortment of Broadway hits, classical pieces, and patriotic songs. Tourists surround the musicians sitting on blankets and munching popcorn or other treats sold nearby. Children run around the gazebo laughing and having a wonderful time with others they just met. At 9 pm sharp the National Anthem is played and the firehouse foghorn sounds, jumping everyone out of their skins. I think it is part of the tradition. This park happens to be located right at the end of Albert Meadow.

At this same park is the hub for the free shuttle system, The Island Explorer. Some of our guests bring bikes and catch the bike express that is part of the shuttle system. This free service takes people to all corners of the island and national park. The bikers head to Eagle Lake where they can access over fifty miles of carriage roads that circle in loops through the interior of the park. These are rustic hard packed gravel roads that are off limits to anything with a motor. They are great for hiking, biking, and horseback riding. The park also has horse drawn carriages available for tours.

The Island Explorer can also drop hikers off at one trailhead and pick them up at a different one. These trails vary in length and in five minutes the hiker can be up the trail enough to get spectacular views. Scores of volunteers help keep these trails in excellent shape. The hikers and bikers leave the drive to the right. The guests with kayaks leave the drive to the left and put in right by Balance Rock. This rock was carried from forty miles away by a glacier many years before. It is often climbed and photographed.

Three year old Gigi visits Grandma often in the summer. She is an early riser like the rest of us so it is a great time to go for a bike or scooter ride. Bar Harbor is just waking up so it is quiet enough for the little speed demon (it is best to get out of her way) to pedal or scoot up Albert Meadow, cross at the crosswalk, ride around the paths in the village park, circle inside the empty gazebo, and head back to Seacroft.

A trip she often takes when the town is very busy is a walk through my parking lot across the street to the miniature horse coral. After a short visit with Chappie and Katie, we proceed up a quiet lane to the chocolate shop. This avoids Main Street when it is bustling. The owners of the shop know Gigi well and she often picks out two small chocolates with her favorite edible topping, sprinkles. We sit outside in the shade of a big moose wearing a bandana and munch on the treats. Those small chocolate fingerprints on the front window belong to my granddaughter.

This chocolate shop also sells local wines so I approached my bridge friends when it was my turn to host to see if they would like to take a small field trip before cards. It was unanimous so off we went on Gigi's route. One lady took multiple pictures of the small horses, and then we moved on to talk with neighbors that everyone knew. We said Hi to a lovable old black Lab that never lacked for attention. At the shop the wine section seemed to be the favorite for the ladies and they purchased a few items. Because of our location we were able to do this without bouncing off tourists on the sidewalks of Main Street.

Acadia National Park, Bar Harbor, and the other towns on Mount Desert Island are special places. We had visited the area many times after we discovered it during our college days. We did not know how special until we lived there and got to really know it. There is the beauty of the environment, the friendliness of its people, the drama of the ocean, the adventure of the wilderness, the liveliness of the towns, the busy life, the simple life, the quiet life, whatever you chose. We also learned to appreciate even more the home and business we chose nearly thirty years before. We have lost some of our ocean views with tree growth but our location is and always will be one of the most appreciated aspects of Seacroft.

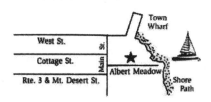

A NON-TRADITIONAL B&B

Since the lodging business is all about its customers, it should be designed with the customer in mind from the very beginning. Of course everyone is an individual and likes different things, but we had to start somewhere. Why not start by designing something that we liked. After staying in a lodging facility we would examine the aspects that we enjoyed. We would incorporate these into our fledgling project. We could always change the things that did not work well later on. There were many changes along the way and there are still many things that could be improved. After nearly thirty years as the Seacroft innkeeper I am proud to say that I am still running the inn and having fun while doing it.

We definitely did not want a traditional B&B. Picture this, a big older home with lots of bedrooms (preferably with private baths), antiques, and common areas shared with the owners, owners who are expected to be on hand to socialize and help with information and directions all hours day and night. We liked our privacy too much to open our home to strangers and this kind of existence. We have watched B&B owners come and go. Since most do share their home in this manner, they get to the point after two or three years where they no longer want to do it.

Guests do not come through our home. There is a desk (remade from an old bureau found in the attic) just inside the front office door where guests register. They then retreat back out through the same door and are shown the coffee room, their parking spaces, and their room entrances. This is the time they might ask their questions but most just want to get to their bathrooms and then on to check out the town and a place to eat. Many cannot be bothered with any information. Seacroft has a large percentage of guests that have been there before and they know more about the island than we do. They come back to Seacroft because they like the same things we do.

So this was the first step to being a non-traditional B&B, not sharing the owners' living quarters. The next step was not having the second B. The traditional places have a full breakfast served at a predetermined time. Guests sit at tables with tablecloths and fine china with other guests, that they may or may not know. The going rate for this more traditional setup is often triple what I charge which represents another non-traditional step, a reasonable rate.

As I mentioned before our rates do not include daily housekeeping or breakfast. If the customer wants either it is available for a reasonable additional fee. Most people are looking for a good deal and if they are willing to do a few things for themselves they save. I know of no other lodging facility that charges extra for housekeeping and breakfast. At the same time I know of no other inn that offers the amenities that we do for such a low rate. It just makes sense and it works for Seacroft. In almost any other business transaction one pays for what he wants and for what he receives. Dave often called our inn, a Blue Collar Inn. We don't advertise it that way but the kind of guests that keep coming are mostly humble, happy, positive, and make an average living. It really doesn't matter what color the collar is.

WHY I WEAR CLOTHES TO BED

While in Norway we stayed in a small apartment with a refrigerator packed with good things to eat during our week's stay. We toyed with this idea for Seacroft since I did not want to prepare breakfasts. But we didn't care for some of the assortment we were offered so why not just furnish the refrigerator and let the guests shop for their own goods.

We didn't want to clean a stove and oven constantly so just furnished a microwave. This allowed guests to reheat their doggy bags but not boil lobster water all over the stovetop. We also furnished a coffeepot, toaster, basic dishes, silverware, wine glasses, bottle opener, paper towels, etc. This has not changed over the years. Guests are not shy about asking for something they might need. I am not shy about saying I do not have that available but I do accommodate every reasonable request. Just recently a guest requested a popcorn bowl, a shot glass, and a soupspoon. How many places supply all of that? Housekeeping cottages might, but generally inns do not even have a mini kitchen.

Another step toward the non-traditional is that we welcome children and have family accommodations. Most of the traditional B&Bs do not allow children under a certain age. I always thought that children are people also and often behave better than their parents. Some people just do not like to deal with children so choose to stay at the more traditional B&Bs for adults. It is nice that there are choices and Bar Harbor has a large number of beds in many different types of lodging.

Seacroft is a unique inn that doesn't appeal to every guest. We always aim to offer a nice product that appeals to the most customers for a very reasonable rate. This we have achieved. For most of our season we have a high if not full occupancy rate. Many nice people come to give us a try, and they often return again and again. They can't all be nice so I will tell you all about the few that weren't. Seasonal customers are called Summer People. I will call the misfits, Some Are Nots!

WHY I WEAR CLOTHES TO BED

SUMMER PEOPLE

SOME ARE NOT

THE EXASPERATING GIANT AND HIS ONLINE GAL

FLYNN FROM FINLAND FRESH OFF THE FERRY

WEDDINGS CAN BE FUN, BUT NOT NECESSARILY FOR THE INNKEEPER

THE LETTER THAT NEVER GOT MAILED

I DON'T HAVE SEIZURES

BRILLIANT PEOPLE OR AT LEAST SMARTER THAN THE AVERAGE

THEY WERE NOT EVEN GUESTS

THREE HOTS AND A COT

THE EXASPERATING GIANT AND HIS ONLINE GAL

The very large man with a very strong guttural accent had called for a reservation. He was from NY and was going to pick his new girlfriend up in Boston on his way to Bar Harbor. He thought this whole trip would take him about 4 hours. He was half right. I think his girlfriend was found through an online dating system. It certainly appeared that they did not know each other well and it was obvious that they really didn't like each other either. He had reserved a room for two nights. They ordered breakfast but never ate it. The baskets came back pretty much full. There was some loud discussion coming from their room but all in all they were okay. They wanted to stay another night but the inn was full. Something told me not to recommend a place to them so I didn't. Call it intuition.

Check out day came and check out time, 11am, came and went with their car still parked in their space. They were not in their room but all of their belongings were. What a mess. I was alone that day since that was the only check out. I was used to cleaning more than one room so this would be easy. Ha! At least it should have been but the room was a disaster. There were his clothes and her clothes everywhere, two open suitcases, toiletries spread out over the bathroom, open wine bottles, burned candles with overflow wax on the furniture, food on every surface, and breakfast still in that morning's basket. An hour after check out time they still had not returned so I went back to the room to start packing up their stuff. A new guest would be coming soon to check into that room. The room had to be clean and ready to give a good first impression.

I didn't know where to start but I tackled the clothes first. If it looked like hers I tossed it into her suitcase and likewise with his. I stripped the bed that was covered with red wine and candle wax. With some tough treating I saved the linens but the pillows had to be tossed out. About the time I started to round up the food the giant guy and his gal returned wondering what I was doing in their room. I reminded them of the check out time. I gave them 15 minutes to vacate the room. They said they might need a little more time than that. I gave them the dirty look that they could interpret anyway they wanted. Giant was upset because I had taken the breakfast basket back to my kitchen on one of my many trips. "I wanted that," he said in his loud and gruff voice. I wrapped up the muffins and bagged everything for traveling. About 30 minutes later they left. It was two hours later that I finally got the room back in order and thoroughly cleaned just in time for the new guests. Hopefully they would never know what had taken place there. I really don't want to know either.

The next day I got a call from an innkeeper who often calls to tell me she has a vacant room. Our inns are comparable in price so it works well to share our last minute vacancies. She started to tell me about this couple that had stayed at Seacroft. I knew exactly whom she was talking about. Unfortunately for this innkeeper it was her inn they had decided to reserve for their last night. I assured her I did not mention her inn to them since I knew she would not want them. While there they were fighting and had gotten louder and louder to the point that the other guests were complaining. True to form they checked out late. They had spilled red wine on an expensive rug, and they left the room devastated. Cleaning up took forever and the rug could not be saved. Apparently this couple was really sick of each other by that third day. I was the lucky one ? to have them the first two days when they were just getting to know each other, and I found them manageable. My innkeeper friend said it was the first time she had ever been afraid of guests that stayed at her inn. She was in tears most of the time they were there and was very happy when they left – until she saw the room. It was then back to tears. The Giant and his Gal proved to be totally insensitive to others and their property. I decided very quickly that a new name would be added to my list of guests who will never return to Seacroft.

FLYNN FROM FINLAND FRESH OFF THE FERRY

Flynn came to Seacroft a long time ago. It was when we still had the ferry coming in every night from Canada, and it was the second year we were open. I have forgotten some of the details but I do remember thinking after just one year in the business I was ready to give it up if there were any more difficult guests like Flynn. The ferry arrived around 10pm and some of the passengers used the six-hour trip to gamble or drink, or both. I know for sure that Flynn was soused when he arrived. He not only smelled strongly of booze but also had the aroma of an ashtray.

The only room we had available was one that we had just opened on the second floor. Since we hadn't yet put an outside entrance and stairway to that room, the guest had to come through our private quarters. We were broke at that time so decided to try this for the summer, and the money we made from it would go toward the new entrance after the season. The guest would require a key to our outside door, but we thought this would be okay since we planned to put just friends and people we knew in it. Strangers with a key made us nervous.

We only allowed Flynn to take the room in the first place because it was late, and the $79 we were charging for the room looked pretty good. The fact that he was leaving on the 8am bus in the morning made it look even more doable. He had asked Dave to make sure he was up in time to take the bus. We thought he would go to bed and sleep it off and that would be it for the evening. There always seems to be a But in this section of my book about errant guests.

Flynn no sooner went to his room than he was out again coming down the spiral staircase. He asked where the nearest bar was and out our door he went. We looked at each other and devised a plan. I would stay up the first half of the night and Dave would take the last half. About midnight he came back with a stranger and they were both climbing the spiral staircase while I watched from the couch. When I spoke they were startled to see me. The other person looked very guilty. I told him he would have to leave since he wasn't registered. He ran down the stairs and didn't look back.

Flynn looked upset and was still very drunk. He said he wasn't ready to go to bed so out he went again. I got Dave up and filled him in. Dave stood guard and was on the couch when Flynn returned with yet another guy. Where did he find these guys in our innocent little Maine town? Dave told them very strongly that there would be no smoking in that room. Little did we know, smoking was the least of our problems.

Later that night there were some interesting sounds coming from their room that could be heard from our 3rd floor bedroom. Sometime in the wee hours the other guy left. At 7am we could not raise Flynn by pounding on the door so Dave went in with the master key and pulled him out of bed. He made sure Flynn got packed and was out in time to catch his bus. Flynn was not helping much in his hung over state.

After Dave guided him out through the front door he staggered off in the right direction.

These guys had quite the party. They had opened the windows and climbed out onto the roof to smoke and drink. There was a big bottle of whiskey tipped over and butts and vomit on the roof. We took this guy in for $79 and it could have cost us thousands. They could have fallen off the roof since they had been drinking a lot. They could have set the inn on fire with their cigarettes.

We lucked out with Flynn and decided we needed to get that outside entrance built sooner than we planned. I had rather not know what our guests are up to, but in this case it was good that we had kept an eye on them. It was particularly good that they were completely separated from the other guests. The outside stairs and new door have worked well for that room over the years. We have never again given a guest a key to the outside door to our private quarters. The Flynn thing discouraged us from doing that and cemented the plan we had made at the very beginning, and that one was to keep our home just for us.

WEDDINGS CAN BE FUN, BUT NOT NECESSARILY FOR THE INNKEEPER

We had just opened and had never had a lodging facility before so were learning as we went. It looked like a busy weekend since we had booked a big wedding party. Our then apartment would house the bride and groom and two of their friends. Four other rooms would also house friends. The rental house next door had ten or twelve others in the wedding party including the parents of the bride. There also must have been thirty or forty friends or family in town for the wedding and were staying elsewhere. This all happened before cell phones. Any calls to the guests had to come through the office. We were taking calls left and right and delivering messages. It became nerve wracking very quickly.

We knew parking would be an issue if the people staying in other hotel facilities drove to our place. And they did since our inn soon became the central meeting place aka the fun house. I had foreseen a parking issue so had told all my guests that if they had visitors they were to park at the end of the street in a public parking lot. The very first night it was pouring and of course no one wanted to walk, not from his or her hotel and not even from the end of the street. I looked out around 8pm and there were cars parked front to back from one end of the front yard to the rear of our property. It was a bottleneck.

"What is it that you don't understand about the parking situation?" I barked. I had gone into the apartment with the bride and groom who were surrounded by at least twenty friends in their small living area. All the happy grins disappeared. It took awhile to clear the driveway out but the problem was never solved the whole weekend.

They had a very rude and pompous friend, Joe the Jerk, who came to visit often and would park anywhere he wanted. I would confront him and he said it was okay since the parking space he took belonged to a friend. Soon the guests whose space it was came back and couldn't use their space so they used someone else's space. This was similar to musical chairs with never enough spaces for the number of cars. It happened time and time again.

The day of the wedding came and there were frantic phone calls, lots of messages to deliver, cars rushing in and out of the driveway, and many near misses. Dave and I were exhausted, completely overwhelmed, and we were not having fun. That night after the wedding was long over, Joe the Jerk returned and since all the parking spaces were full, he left his car right under my window completely blocking the driveway. This, of course, woke me up so I could again feel my blood pressure rising. Hatred is a strong word but it described what I felt about this arrogant being. As I lay there wide-awake and very angry, I could hear that both the house next door and our inn were in party mode. I looked forward to tomorrow. Thankfully they would all be gone.

The next day everyone left way after check out time and the rooms were a mess. Luckily for us one of our daughters was there to help us get them ready for the turnaround. The friends of the bride and groom left without paying, and stuck them with the entire bill. Some friends! I could tell by the expressions on the newlyweds' faces that they did not expect this even though they had secured all the rooms with their credit card.

Unlike so many guests, these folks never returned. I never knew what happened to them. I often wondered if this couple stayed together and if they ever forgave their friends for leaving without offering to help with the inn bill. No one was very happy with us since we were always trying to correct all the wrongs going on. We then knew without a doubt that we were not set up for weddings because we had a bad phone set up and just enough parking for our registered guests. We turned down many requests after that incident.

Times have changed and we have since had many groups, family reunions, and weddings at Seacroft. I determine who is willing to take charge in the group to keep things on an even keel. I deal with that one person, I find out what they need from me, and I tell them what I need from them. Most important of all, they cannot disturb the other guests. This means a reasonable time to stop partying. Parking is not a big issue any more since we purchased a lot across the road, too small for a building lot but just right for a parking lot. Cell phones are really handy when there are friends and family all over town who need to communicate. In room landline phones are no longer necessary so have been removed.

Just recently I was happy to help out with a small wedding that took place in my coffee room. Two nice girls wanted very badly to get married but didn't want a big affair. They had too many friends where they lived to keep the wedding small and private so decided to find a beautiful spot far away for their special day. They researched states other than their own that sanctioned same sex marriages. They brought their pastor and her wife but another person was needed as a witness. I was asked and proudly accepted. I was also asked to take pictures. They had a lovely meaningful ceremony designed just for them. There were a lot of happy tears and smiles. Weddings aren't so bad after all, but that first one was a doozy.

THE LETTER THAT NEVER GOT MAILED!

Sometimes people are insensitive to others, and some of those people are smokers! Thankfully it seems that there are a lot less smokers now than there used to be.

People have become more health conscience. Some try to give up the habit and have success. Others are so addicted they had just rather smoke and deal with the consequences if and when they come. The problem is that bad consequences happen to innocent bystanders by way of secondhand smoke. It is a nasty unhealthy habit. Even the smell of the smoke is offensive to nonsmokers.

When we first opened in the early 90's as a nonsmoking inn, I actually had guests that would smoke in their rooms thinking they could get away with it. They didn't realize I could detect cigarette smoke from someone walking down the street one hundred yards away or on the highway from someone smoking in the car in front of me. There would be ashes on a windowsill where one would smoke by an open window. Sometimes guests would smoke on the deck near open windows. You might as well be smoking in nearby rooms as the smoke would inevitably drift in.

My decks are now posted with No Smoking signs. When guests check in, those that smoke stand out because of the aroma on their breaths and clothes. I often will ask them to please smoke off the premises. Some actually look surprised that I know they are smokers. They shouldn't be surprised since they have to know that telltale scent follows them everywhere. Okay, that is quite enough about smokers smelling badly.

There was a couple that roared in on motorcycles and took a room with a deck. They were only at the inn for two nights but when we went into the room after they checked out, we were hit with that horrible smell. The smoke seemed to permeate into every crevice. My detection system must have been off kilter those days. One of my daughters was visiting so had volunteered to clean like she always does. She helped Kady and me strip everything out of the room for laundering that could be laundered.

It appeared that these guests had smoked on the deck with the windows to the room wide open. Not only that but they were running the AC which was sucking the smoke into the room and circulating it. We cleaned for 3 hours, sprayed bottles of air freshener, dragged fans into the room, changed the AC filters, and cleaned the plastic trashcans. Every surface had to be wiped down and sprayed. The more the three of us worked the closer I got to my boiling point.

The couple that was scheduled to come into the room that day would never tolerate a room that smelled like smoke. It took the three of us well over three hours to do everything we could to get the room clean. We got the room as good as we knew how and fortunately it was good enough for the repeat customers that took it over. It was time to let the smokers know about the work they had caused us. I wrote a two-page letter telling them how disappointed I was in them for causing the extreme intrusion from their smoking. They had stayed in an ultra clean room in a nonsmoking inn and smoked steadily on a posted deck. They had carelessly left the AC on and the windows open circulating smoke into every corner. They had caused us to work many extra hours to get the room clean for a couple that did not smoke and would never stay in a room where there had been smokers.

I accused them of being insensitive to others with their nasty habit. This habit not only was an annoyance but a health hazard. I said if they had just taken a walk when they smoked, and dropped their butts in the trashcan at the end of the street, they would be doing us and everybody else a huge favor. I certainly understand why some inns charge $200 or more to the guest that smokes in a nonsmoking room. It would barely cover the cleaning expenses.

Writing this letter made me feel better and I was convinced that the guilty ones would learn from it. I had the envelope stamped and ready to send but wanted my kids to read the letter first. They knew what the cleaning had entailed and knew how I felt. They all thought the letter would do no good and I definitely should not send it. I wasn't sure why but I did what they suggested. I did not mail the letter. However, there was one thing I could do about it. There were new names on my List of People that Will Never Return to Seacroft, and they did try.

I DON'T HAVE SEIZURES

If someone comes right out and says I don't have something, he usually does have that something. Frank stopped by one day on the chance I had a vacancy. I happened to have one night available so he took it. He didn't appear to feel very well but soon after checking in he was off. He came back several hours later and told me about his adventures. He mentioned stopping here and there, having a cocktail or two, and sleeping them off before he could drive further on. He looked very tired and said he was turning in early.

The next day he planned to leave and I made sure he knew that check out time was 11 am. At 10:45 he called me to tell me he would be late getting out of his room. He wasn't feeling well so thought he would take a quick shower. A little after 11:30 am he came to the office with blood and bruises on his face and arms. He was feeling badly about breaking a towel rack and for getting blood on the sheets and towels and apologized profusely. I really wasn't concerned about the towel rack or the blood. We are used to treating the laundry for blood stains since many of our guests get minor wounds biking and hiking. I was really concerned about him. He had told me he did not have seizures but he had gotten light headed getting out of the shower and had simply fallen which broke the towel rack when he grabbed it.

He had talked with his brother for over 3 hours that morning asking him what he should do since he wasn't sure he should drive. He apparently had some condition that his brother was aware of and he often called him to get counseling and help with decisions. Kady was here so she took over the cleaning and I took care of Frank. He was shaking and I didn't want him to start driving somewhere.

He did not want coffee so I made him some tea and sat with him awhile in the sun on the front lawn. He was clearly agitated. I wanted to talk with his brother but he didn't want me to. I had to do some inn chores so left him there on the lawn to rest. His phone needed charging so I did not think he would suddenly take off without it.

I kept an eye out and noticed he had moved from the chair to the grass. I thought that he was napping since he had not slept well.

A few minutes later a passerby came to the office and said the man on the lawn was convulsing. I grabbed my phone and called an ambulance. It arrived shortly just as he was coming to. He was incoherent and told the paramedics that he had not fallen when they asked him. I think he meant he had not fallen on the lawn. I told them that he had fallen in the bathroom which caused his bruises. His phone was lying beside him so I tried to find his brother's number. The phone was coded so I couldn't, but I gave it to the paramedics who whisked him off to the nearby hospital.

After the ambulance left with my guest in tow I noticed his car keys on the grass where he had been lying. I pocketed them and felt safe that he would not be driving that day. His rental car was parked in the spot that a registered guest would soon need.

I called the hospital later on to find out what I could

about Frank but with privacy issues I didn't find out a thing. I told his nurse that I had his car keys and I was really concerned that he would be released and would try to drive. She said he would not be driving. She called later to say that the rental company would soon be picking up the car, and that the patient was being transferred to the Bangor hospital.

I often don't know how these stories turn out but I often wondered why this man had a license and was allowed to rent a car since he obviously was not well enough to drive. I surmised that he was on some kind of medication and had admitted to drinking. That very well could have been a trigger for his problems that day. Even though he said he did not have seizures he had something very similar and was a long way from home without family to help him. I can only hope the hospital could help him find his very long road back.

BRILLIANT PEOPLE OR AT THE LEAST SMARTER THAN THE AVERAGE

Have you ever known a really bright person who seemed to have a small amount of common sense? After nearly 30 years in this business I have met a lot of people from all walks of life. My guests have included doctors, college professors, and lab researchers. I enjoy talking with them and hearing about their professions. Occasionally I get really surprised by some simple things that I thought they could easily handle but couldn't, or at least didn't.

There used to be venetian blinds in one guest room that could be manipulated with long strings for lowering and raising. I learned very fast not to put my lab scientists in that room. It took me ages to get those knotted and tangled strings straightened out after their visits. It seemed that these lab guests could handle the big life changing projects but did not have the patience to figure out the blind mechanism. It wasn't long before I just put these important people in a different room. And it wasn't long after that I replaced the blinds with something more foolproof.

One day outside of one room there was a very large pile of soaking wet towels. A college professor had obviously not put her shower curtain inside the tub before showering. Confident that she would do just that the next day I did not mention it. The next day, however, there it was, a sopping pile of towels just like the day before. She not only did it once but did the very same thing the second day. This time I asked her to put the shower curtain inside the tub before showering. Her only comment was, "Oh!"

Another college professor who was not a guest but a coworker of Dave's at the University asked him about his license plate. We had special Maine plates at the time and used them to advertise. Limited to seven characters on the vanity plates, mine said, "Seacrof" and Dave's said, "CCROFT." The professor had visited us in Bar Harbor and was familiar with our inn. He was studying Dave's plate for quite awhile one day and finally asked him, "Who is C C Roft?" This man had a brilliant mind, wrote heady articles in national educational magazines, and could read one thing and talk about something else at the same time but couldn't decipher the name on the license plate.

A guest who had a PhD and lived in D. C. did important research for the government. She asked me what I thought of Global Warming. I told her I thought it was a serious issue but the positive thing about it was that I would be waterfront in a few thousand years. I asked her if that was the topic of her research and she said NO, it was because she was extremely afraid of alligators and snakes and was concerned that they would move north and become a nuisance where she lived in D. C. I thought this sounded a bit unusual coming from a very smart lady.

I don't mean to stereotype here but I did see the irony in this happening over and over. I, of course, realize that many brilliant people can handle the small stuff. Dave was a college professor and taught many students. He had an amazing amount of common sense and could relate to his students no matter what their backgrounds were. Dave could handle the small stuff but I still relied on him to take care of the big issues.

One day a guest came to the office with a very big problem. His key did not work and he could not get into his room. I tried my master key and a room key and the lock was completely frozen. I was about to call a locksmith when the door opened from the inside. Dave had scaled a ladder to the second floor, opened a window on the other side of the room, and had climbed in. He quickly fixed the lock by tightening some screws. Crisis was averted, a combination of a big and little problem solved by a man who was both a college professor that touched many lives and a handyman who could fix the simple things.

THEY WERE NOT EVEN GUESTS

This incident took a lot of my time and none of my efforts seemed to help these people. There is no doubt in my mind that this couple should be safely tucked away from the rest of society instead of out on the roads endangering lives, and they definitely should not be at my inn making demands of me.

This deranged woman, I will call her Jo, came bursting into the office and asked if she was registered at the inn. The other half of this couple, known as Carl, did not show up until later. Jo said she had a reservation somewhere and couldn't remember where. She knew it was a 4 star hotel and she thought our little seven room inn must be one of them.

Kady called all the 4 star facilities that we knew about and none had her registered ------ so they said. Jo had a husband somewhere in town but she couldn't remember where she dropped him off. She said he was "just stomping around out there." She had a dog so I thought she must be staying at a pet friendly facility. She actually said the hotel did not accept dogs but would take her small one for $75. a night. I guess money was not an issue.

She kept saying her husband said it was Harbor

38

something where they were supposed to be staying but she knew that wasn't right. We had called all the 4 star places starting with Harbor and they had said they did not have anyone registered by that name. After asking many questions and making many calls I told Jo I did not know how to help her anymore.

She had wandered into the living room several times looking around which is a no no. I finally told her that was private and she would have to leave so I could get to work. She didn't leave but sat in the chair by the door in a very agitated state where I kept an eye on her. Eventually she went to her car parked in a guest spot at the front of the inn.

She was still there 30 minutes later, so I asked her what her problem was and there seemed to be quite a few. She said she couldn't get the car started and asked me to call AAA. I asked her where her key fob was and she had no idea what I was talking about but she looked for it anyway - all around where she was sitting. I could tell it was a keyless access car like mine and she needed the key fob within 5 feet of the car for it to start. She didn't seem to understand that and said it always started right up before. I surmised that Carl must have possessed the key fob and he was amongst the missing.

I asked more questions, and made more calls. I was calling the same places as before but this time I was getting the same recorded message from all of them. They were all 4 star owned by the same management and apparently were not taking any calls at that time - at least not on the 800# lines. I told Jo I would call a policeman to help her. She thought that was a great idea because she really needed help.

A very nice local policeman showed up quickly. Jo told him a completely different story than she told me. The cop and I did the eye roll that acknowledged we both thought she was nuts. He got some info on her husband and went looking for him. I finally called the local # to the hotel rather than the elusive 800# where I thought they might be staying even though we had called them before. This time I actually got a desk person, and found out that the long lost husband was there. This time they said that yes, this couple was registered there. Just then the cop came back so I asked him to get the key fob from the hubby so she could get out of my parking space and to her hotel. I believe he thought the husband had to be better suited to drive than Jo was so he said he would get both Carl and the key. Big Mistake!

Hubby got there and he was worse off than she was - physically, mentally, and emotionally. They started yelling at each other and the cop was afraid they were going to start punching. We both had noticed a big bruise on her face. He looked at me and I just shrugged. I had nothing to offer that would help. He got them to settle down and he thought they were all set so left.

But they were not all set. They got the car started but it refused to budge. Dan, a guest, tried to help, but he got rudely yelled at so retreated back to his room. He later said, "They aren't coming back here are they?"

I called the police station a second time and a different cop came. After awhile he could move the car. I am not sure what the problem was but I think it might have had an automatic anti theft device since she had been trying to start it for over an hour - without the key fob. He could see that neither of them were in any shape to drive when Carl backed into the rosebush and Jo did just as poorly when she took her turn behind the wheel. He asked them both to sit in back with the dog and he drove them to their hotel. I was relieved when I saw the tail end of their car finally leaving Seacroft.

I wanted to talk with the cop but I did not catch him in time when he came back to get his car. This all took about 3 hours of my afternoon. This sad and very unstable couple got here somehow from southern Maine but it was clear that neither was capable of driving safely. I hope the cop could do something about that. I do not know how this story ended but I may find out in the next Police Beat.

(Note - This story never showed up in the newspaper. The Police Beat often had comical and unusual stories. I believe the reporter for the Police Beat felt extremely sorry for this couple and saw nothing funny about it. I think of Carl and Jo often and hope they are back safely where they can be assisted. I did not find them very endearing but I certainly did not wish them any harm. I am a dog lover and I can say the dog was great.)

THREE HOTS AND A COT

That was the name Kady's Dad gave to a jail cell, Three Hots and a Cot. It played a big part in Gil's stay at Seacroft. One day shortly after I opened the inn for the season a big burly guy came into my office and asked about staying for a night at the inn. He was full of positives, loving the town, the park, and the people, just about everything. After checking out his room he came back and paid for two more nights because he loved the inn, the street, and the location near the ocean.

When I was watering my plants on the deck he wandered by and started talking about himself. He said he was an actor, a mime, and a singer. He thought he could find a job that came with housing and meals. I told him not to count on that. But he had talked to a woman in a store and she had lucked out with a job and the benefits that he was looking for. He thought a front desk job was something he might try.

He did not appear to have nice clothes and he smelled like booze. I did not think he had a chance of finding any kind of job. The first night he drove out of the yard and found his first pub. He told me the next day he had to sleep it off in his car because he couldn't remember how to get back to the inn. He found us early the next morning and took a shower and asked me to launder his clothes. I do laundry for guests for a small fee so they don't have to waste their vacation time at a laundromat. His clothes were in rough shape covered in mold and paint that of course did not come out but at least they were a whole lot cleaner. He enjoyed his inn robe and could be seen in the coffee room with not only the robe but also a bandana around his neck, a sweatband around his head, and possibly nothing else.

He asked me for more lotion because he had run out of it softening his feet. I don't supply lotion so knew he was putting shampoo on his feet. Instead of giving him more shampoo I found some lotion that probably worked better. He was still loving everything that morning and said he was going to check out the park and look for a job.

Gil said a policeman had stopped him for having a broken headlight. The car was a mess, a real clunker, and had more issues than the headlight. He had hand painted stripes on it to look like an animal. He told me the cop had given him a breathalyzer test. Even with clean clothes he unfortunately still smelled like booze.

I lost track of him that day. His car was back in my parking space right next to a BMW. I thought they looked like a rather comical pair. Gil, however, was nowhere to be seen. He must have walked to a bar or somewhere else in town. On his check out day he was still nowhere in sight but all of his belongings were still in his room. Kady and I put everything in his laundry bag and duffle. Amongst his things was one shoe, medicine, and two big open bottles of booze. His car was locked up but the window was wide open so we could pack all his belongings into the back seat.

After checking with the local police I found out he was in jail - which of course explained why he was not around. They also told me he was about to make bail so I thought he would of course come and get his car and possessions.

Gil also had a key to the room that was about to belong to someone else. I had it reserved for a new couple but I had to recommend that they go to another inn. They agreed after I told them why. Sending them away cost me $200 but I did not want this inebriated character to unlock their door in the middle of the night. New locks and keys for the room cost me another $100.

Then I found out from a different source that he did not make bail and was still in jail. I had no choice but to have his car towed and impounded. I never heard from him again but he made the Police Beat twice for disturbing the peace and for DUI.

From the conversations with him when he was close to sober, I surmised that he was an intelligent man but could not leave alcohol alone and could not act appropriately while drinking. He never got a job in the place he loved but he got the free meals and room that he had been looking for, or as Kady's dad would say, Three Hots and a Cot.

AND WHAT IS YOUR SPECIALTY?

Talk about special guests! Special people make special guests. Rob and Cheryl are the best and I can't imagine anyone disliking them. They truly love and respect each other and I enjoy spending time with happy couples that never seem to argue. Rob recently retired and Cheryl could work long distance so they moved to a new state closer to Bar Harbor. They have been coming for years, for a week in the spring and a week or more in the fall. I have gotten to know them quite well over the years.

I really got to know them after I spotted Rob on my roof. He thought he would help me out by cleaning out my gutters. I in turn thought it would be fun to take them out to eat. We quickly became friends beyond the usual guest and inn owner relationship. After I treated them they thought they ought to take me out to dinner and for several years we have taken turns treating each other. They have a great sense of humor and spending time with them is a delight.

Whenever they come they ask me if I have a list of chores for them to do. I try not to take too much of their time since they are on vacation but something always seems to pop up where they can really help me out. They are both IT people and they have helped me with computer issues and with setting up TV's and DVD's.

Cheryl planned a Christmas card for me with pictures of my new granddaughter using her Power Point program. During the last visit Rob installed new doorknobs when I needed my locks changed. If I don't have anything on my list they create one if they see something they can do to help.

One morning in the coffee room I was talking with them about all their talents and help around the inn. I mentioned I should ask every guest what his or her specialty is. A new guest sitting with his newspaper was apparently listening and said when he got back from his hike he would paint since he was really good at that. He was very serious about helping. I told him I would list that specialty on his card for the future. Situations like this make me think of my guests as friends and my inn as a Home Away from Home for them.

I am not much of a drinker but when there are friends and wine I really like a glass. Rob and Cheryl will sit on the deck late afternoon to relax after a day of hiking Acadia. Cheryl knits and Rob reads or they just chat about their day. They often share a bottle of wine with other guests and me. If I am not outside Rob will come to the office to pour me a glass. They even offered to help me out with a personal matter that involved driving in Boston to and from the hospital. That was very much appreciated since I do not drive in Boston.

It appears that I am not the only one they help. In their new location they have used their love of animals to help out at a nearby No Kill shelter. They organize fund drives as well as spend time doing whatever has to be done whether it is bottle feeding a baby goat or building a barn. Rob retired from his paying job but now volunteers more than forty hours a week, mostly with farm animals. The shelter takes in any critter that needs a home whether it be horses, chickens, lamas, goats, dogs, cats or you name it.

Cheryl blogs about many of the animals and is instrumental in finding the right pet for the right home. If

I remember correctly she wrote about a goose that was placed on a University Campus to keep some other animal company.

Also there was Fiona, a pot bellied pig who was an escape artist. She would often make a break for it and run away. She liked to eat so would seek out humans with pig food. These folks knew all about Fiona and would return her to the shelter. It was up to Rob to design a new pen that not only kept her in but kept her from getting bored. After he made a solid wooden pen he put rocks in the bottom. Her food was placed under the rocks so she would keep busy digging around to find her meals. Fiona quickly found an excellent Forever Home and kept her new owners on their toes with her unusual habits.

Rob also got involved with an illegal Rooster Fighting Ring. He had to leave Seacroft a day early on one of their visits when the police asked him to accompany them on breaking up the Ring. Rob was asked to help out because he was known as a skillful rooster catcher. I hope he didn't have to catch all four hundred of the roosters involved.

I enjoy reading about the shelter through Cheryl's eyes and hearing stories about these animals up close and personal. The lives of these animals have been vastly improved by Rob and Cheryl and many others just like them. This couple has many specialties and those talents would make a very long list. I am a lucky innkeeper to have guests like Rob and Cheryl, but I am even luckier to have them as my good friends.

A VERY SPECIAL GUEST

Barry was one of my many really good guests. Having grown up in Bar Harbor, he enjoyed coming to the high school reunions in August. He and his wife May had always stayed in one of the original motels from the 50's, but May was ready to make a change. When Barry was off fishing or meeting up with old friends she walked around town and found us. She apparently told Barry where they would be staying the next year. I am not sure what he said at the time but I suspect he wanted to stay at the same motel down the street. He later told me he was glad she decided to make the change. He loved our place.

The first three years of his stay here, Barry would follow Dave around outside and listen to his jokes and stories. I heard him laughing one day and he said, "That was worth the price of my room any day." I was outside chatting with Barry and May one day and Dave joined us and put his arm around my shoulders. We both noticed that Barry's jaw dropped a foot. For a while he remained speechless. Barry had never realized we were a married couple. He looked at Dave and stammered, "I thought you were the handyman!" For some reason he never put the two of us together. I guess we were usually busy doing our own chores.

It was a standing joke after that. Dave was called the handyman. We made up some tee shirts with a picture of Seacroft on them. Each one was personalized with a nickname. Mine was Boss, Dave's was of course Handyman, and Barry had his own matching shirt that said Special Guest. Every visit after that when he arrived he was wearing his Special Guest shirt.

When I had time and Barry was sitting still long enough he would tell stories of his childhood in Bar Harbor. He was disappointed that he could no longer get a burger and shake for a quarter. At seventeen he lied about his age and went off to war in the Navy where he soon captained a ship that supplied our fighting men in Europe. He talked about squeezing though a narrow cave-like channel off the Mediterranean with just inches on each side of his big ship. There were also tales about many topics. I was not to mention his wartime girlfriends to May but there were a few stories about them also.

Soon Barry and May brought family that filled more of our rooms. They all raved about the blueberry muffins so when they were here I was doing some baking. I did have to occasionally serve something else and many guests liked bagels. The morning we had those Barry could not contain himself. He said he could not eat that piece of dried up bread. It was not the first time he made his wishes known but most of the time he was ecstatic to be here and in his hometown. I made him some homemade toast and jam, which was acceptable. I never put bagels in his basket again but it didn't stop me from threatening to do so.

Barry became ill as he approached his 90's and sadly passed away. May and his family still come to Seacroft. They always go to his favorite spots, take their blueberry muffins in a picnic basket, and reminisce about their very special guy. It has been several years since I have seen Barry and I still miss him very much. One of my fondest memories of any guest is Barry rushing through the office door wearing a great big grin and his Special Guest tee shirt from Seacroft.

A FOLLOW UP WITH MAY

I am writing this right after May visited Seacroft with part of her family. A year had gone by since Barry passed away. I gave her the first draft of the section about her husband, Barry, and I was anxious to get her reaction. Being a nice person she said she loved it, but wanting to be honest about it she needed to make a correction. She said the ship that Barry navigated through the narrow cave was really quite small and not the big ship he had described to me. This is not really that important but it was an example of the embellishment that Barry added to his stories. Her son in law who was listening to our conversation said that it was the Flavor of Barry's stories that was important and not the Facts. I had been very careful so far to use Facts as I knew them while writing about Seacroft. As they say, I have changed the names to protect the innocent, but I will continue my writing journey with Flavor in mind and feel free to possibly make minor changes in some of the Facts. If Barry, a great storyteller, could do it, I can also. May also told me that she had donated much of her husband's belongings to charity but one of the few things she will always keep of Barry's is his Special Guest tee shirt from Seacroft.

LOST IN THE WOODS WITH BUNNY BROWN

Vera has been a guest at Seacroft for nearly twenty years, and a good friend for about the same length of time. She is a retired critical care nurse from Missouri. Little did she know when she was planning her first trip to New England that she would end up coming every fall after that. She is not only my friend but she and Kady are good friends also and share a love for the local greasy spoon. They often have breakfast together before Kady comes to work. Kady says everyone there knows Vera, and Kady, the local, is known as Vera's friend. Vera, Kady, and I often go out for dinner when the inn is quiet. There is never a break in our conversation.

I love to hike but I also love to just tend the inn so the later usually takes priority. When Vera is around she and I go for short hikes when I can get away. It is a great time to catch up on each other's lives.

This past fall Vera read a few excerpts from my memoirs and got the idea that I should write about our latest hike. She even titled it for me, Lost in the Woods with Bunny Brown. I never use the word Lost since I always know where I am even though I may not be where I planned to be. This has happened in the past when family members or friends get talking and we miss a sign.

Many years ago when Dave, Tammy, and I climbed the Precipice we intended to descend on a trail that would get us back to our car. We of course got lost in conversation and ended up going down the backside of the mountain. We realized our mistake about half way down and decided to keep going. We had to walk two extra miles to Seacroft to get our second car in order to retrieve the first car where we had left it on the other side of the mountain. Another time Tammy and I drifted accidentally from the Kebo Trail to a different one. I looked around and knew we were now on the Gorge Trail. It was no biggie; it just took a little longer to return to our car. As I said, I was not lost; I was just not where I planned to be. It should be noted that this all happened before we had the benefit of the Island Explorer.

Planning a fun morning hike in Acadia is always easy with lots of choices. I knew Vera would be game for anything. We would take the Island Explorer to Jordan Pond, hike through the woods of Acadia, meander through beautiful gardens, descend terraces overlooking the harbor, and end up at a favorite restaurant before catching the shuttle back to Bar Harbor. My only excuse for missing the garden trail was lack of signage.

We walked in a big circle, tried again, and finally headed toward a major route in Seal Harbor. I wasn't lost in the sense that I knew we were headed in the right direction and we were on a carriage road between Little Long Pond and the gardens. I knew the gardens were to our right but chose not to take any of the rough unmarked trails in that direction. The hike turned out to be a lot longer than I anticipated. It was very pretty walk along Somes Sound on the paved highway but we encountered a lot of traffic making the last two mile stretch unpleasant.

We resolved to try again next year and take the correct

trail that is two miles shorter than the highway route. We never got physically tired, never ran out of conversation, and never worried about being lost. At least I wasn't worried about being lost. When Vera sent the suggestion for this story she did title it Lost in the Woods with Bunny Brown; so come to think of it she might have been a wee bit worried about being lost. I love Vera and we share some great stories. I would have titled this one a Mighty Adventure, since it is about as adventuresome as two old ladies can get.

THE LITTLE LOST BOY

Donny came running into the office one afternoon crying hysterically. Through the tears and sobs he told me that he had lost his mommy and daddy in a toy store. There are multiple stores with toys so I would not pursue that route. I calmed him down and told him we would find his parents quickly. I told him I would call the police because I was sure his parents would also. I am not sure what store he came from but for his age, around six, he did well to find Seacroft where his family was staying.

Before I could call the police, I heard a door bang and someone running up the stairs in another part of the inn. I smiled at Donny and said, "I bet that is your daddy now looking for you." We rushed out the office door and in through the door that led to their room. Racing down the stairs was a very worried dad. They probably hadn't been separated for more than fifteen minutes but the big hug reunion was something to witness. I am not sure why but I was tearing up along with them.

After they realized Donny was out of sight and they couldn't find him anywhere in the store Dad called the police. Mom had stayed at the store in case Donny came back or was still there somewhere. Dad knew Donny well

56

and headed to Seacroft running the whole way. After finding Donny he quickly called both the police and Mom to relay the good news. He thanked me profusely for everything I did which wasn't much.

There are horror stories of what can happen to children that get separated from their parents in stores and malls, but nothing bad like that has ever happened in our safe little Maine town.

I had always told our children if we ever got separated in a crowd they should just stop right where they are when they realized we were out of sight. It happened only once. It was our first trip to Disney World and there was so much to see that was different and exciting. Our two youngest who were six and eight at the time were suddenly out of sight. We backtracked and found them quickly right where we had been a few minutes before. We were relieved to have found them so quickly and proud and pleased that they had done as we had asked.

I am not sure what they had discussed as a family if they ever got into this situation but Dad told Donny he was so proud of him for finding his way back to Seacroft. I am not sure many children his age could have done that.

I have always loved children and they are certainly welcome at Seacroft. It is nice to see families enjoying the wonders of Acadia and the fun activities that Bar Harbor has to offer. Hopefully Donny will someday find his way back to Seacroft just as he had done years before when he was just a little lost boy.

SAM AND JANIE, THE PERFECT COUPLE

They are another couple that love and respect each other. They married late and never had children, and some couples are perfect just the way they are.

When Seacroft was very young, Janie came as a guest with two of her college friends. We liked her personality from the very beginning. She was always positive and happy and seemed to be the group leader. They had not seen each other for a few years since after college they had all gone in different directions. Janie ended up in California and was the only one still single. Needless to say there was a great deal of laughter coming from their room. They loved Seacroft and made a pact that any future trips to Bar Harbor would include Seacroft and would be just for the girls.

Nearly thirty years later, much has happened in Janie's life, and it mostly has to do with Sam. Janie ended up teaching at a small college near Pasadena. One day she was walking to work and spotted a guy about her age riding his bike in the same direction. When he passed her she noticed he had a great looking "tushy", her own words. After that Janie and Sam ran into each other often since they worked at the same college. They were both single and noticed that they had a lot in common. They both had multiple interests and were always seeking knowledge about everything, especially if it were about the environment.

Sam was a scientist and worked as a seismologist. California is a good place to be if you want to learn more about earthquakes. It turns out that Sam is an expert in just about everything scientific. Sam and Janie quickly became a couple and soon married. Janie wanted to share Bar Harbor with him but because of the pact she had to get the girls to okay Seacroft. Janie laughed when she told me they quickly gave her permission since she was so hard up for a boyfriend at the time. So we got to meet them both and were really impressed with them. As I said before Special People make Special Guests. Special Guests become Special Friends.

Over the years Sam and Janie made many long trips east to stay at Seacroft, hike Acadia, and visit with east coast family. Computers became important during that time and we discovered that Sam also had expert knowledge of those that of course was not surprising. We enlisted him to help us with all of the technical issues that we experienced, and there were quite a few. We would apologize for taking so much of his vacation time and Janie would always smile and say he loves to figure these things out.

About ten years ago Sam and Janie moved east and built one of the first solar homes in the area. They have a room with a command center needed for their set up. The details made my head spin when they were describing it. Their home sits on several acres near a river and they raise a lot of their own food. They live inexpensively and completely off the grid. Every year they make an extensive and sometimes unusual trip to some far off place they want to learn more about such as Iceland, Alaska, Africa,

China, Australia, and Antarctica. Sam is also an expert photographer and takes gorgeous and often unusual pictures.

It is so nice to have them in the area and to see them often. Even today whenever I need computer help, Sam and Janie come to the rescue. The computer problems don't take long to conquer so we end up chatting for hours. One of the things we all enjoy is dining at Geddy's and having their delicious fish fry. That has become a tradition both spring and fall whether the computer needs to be dealt with or not. As I mentioned before it is fun to share time with a happy couple that truly enjoys each other. I know I can always count on them at any time to help me out if I need it. I never put them on my Specialty list because it would require a Santa sized piece of paper. Their extensive knowledge of so many topics is amazing. Watching Jeopardy makes me feel pretty dumb, but my bet is that they would do very well on that show.

TASHA AND KITTY, HECKLE AND JECKLE

Before there were Kitty and Heckle and Jeckle, there was Tasha. Tasha was also from the west coast and is Sam's sister. She would often come with Sam and Janie and was a guest in the next room. When they got in close proximity of each other they were like the Three Stooges, always telling funny stories and playing pranks. They took great pride in keeping their rooms neat so I would tell each one in secret that he or she was my favorite guest. Soon they were playing pranks on Dave and me. They were always offering us a potato for lunch but we were on guard against the inevitable dirty deed. One of the meals they prepared frequently to save money consisted of Maine baked potatoes nuked in their microwave. There was never a dull moment when the three of them were together.

Tasha was a fireman or I should say firewoman. She was very strong and I am sure could keep up with the others when it came to climbing ladders, wielding hoses, and making rescues. It no doubt was a stressful job but when she was here with her brother and sister in law she was just having fun. She soon fell in love with this area and moved here as soon as she could retire. She bought a huge piece of property on a lake near Sam and Janie and built a solar house similar to theirs. She too is a brilliant person and very knowledgeable about the environment and computers.

When she made the move she brought her partner Kitty. They drove their own moving truck across country and did all the loading and unloading by themselves. The family became united and I can only hope they behave more maturely now than when they were guests at the inn, but I am guessing they don't.

Tasha and Kitty had planned to get two black labs as soon as they settled into their new home. They even designed a doggie room with a door to the outside and a pet friendly tub and shower. It wasn't long before they found a couple of darling and active lab mixes and named them Heckle and Jeckle. These dogs have a dream life living on the lake where they have learned to doggy dive off the wharf, stand up paddleboard, kayak with their mistresses, and they have the run of fifty acres. Every Christmas I am the recipient of a gorgeous calendar with pictures of Heckle and Jeckle posing in action doing their favorite activities. Kitty is clever at making entertaining videos of the pooches doing their thing with background music. These dogs enjoy the best that life can offer. People should have it so good.

I don't have this crew as guests any more since they live nearby. They all have their special skills but the best one of all is that they are just plain nice. Sam and Janie visit and help me with the computer. The ladies help me out by picking up my cans and bottles. It is a big job to sort, clean, and turn in for the little bit of cash. They are helping the environment and they use the cash for purchasing dog toys at Bark Harbor. We often reminisce of the olden days at Seacroft. It is my privilege to know and love this family.

THE TCHOTCHKE AND THE POEM

The Tchotchke I am writing about is a figurine of a comedic hen with a spoon and pot and a rooster hiding his eyes behind his wings. It was labeled, "Dave and Bunny, Innkeepers of the Year." About seven years after Sam, Janie, and Tasha started coming to the inn they presented this to us with great flair. The tchotchke still sits on the shelf over my kitchen sink where I can see it every day. It represents the friends I have made and the fun that I have running Seacroft. I have to share the poem written by the Three Stooges that came with the tchotchke. Keep in mind the authors are scientifically minded so are all Left Brained. Left brained folks know their science but are not gifted in composing poetry. Don't try to make a lot of sense out of it.

T'was the Week before Halloween
When all through the Inn
The Couple in Room 3
Was raising a Din.
When to the Rescue
Came the Resident in Room 2
Then she soon Discovered

WHY I WEAR CLOTHES TO BED

There was too Much to Do.
There was Banging and Clanging
And Dust on the Floor
There were empty Coffee Cups
 And so much more......
The Towels were all Wet
The Bedding Askew
Oh this isn't Room 3
This is Room 2!
Then came Bunny and Dave
The Vacuum a Flying
An Arm full of Towels
Which Stopped all the Crying
With a fresh Cup of Coffee
And a T-shirt or few
They got the Residents of 3
Talking to 2
Many thanks are in Order
For the Innkeepers here
And in Addition an Award
For "Innkeepers of the Year"

While the authors of the poem were visiting recently, I brought it forth to share with them. They enjoyed reading it after all these years and laughed recalling the racket they raised while guests.

It's not Walt Whitman, but I love it. Sam, Janie, and Tasha took the time to create these rhymes to let us know we were appreciated. That meant a lot to us to know we must be doing something right.

ANNIE AND HER EXES

Annie is a great lady with many wonderful attributes and a perfect and persistent smile. She is also on the lookout for a nice guy who likes the same things that she likes. She comes every year and always brings a friend, a relative, or in most cases an ex boyfriend. Annie loves to hike our trails in Acadia, but the men she brings are not physical enough to keep up with her and do not even have the desire to hike. They seem to just be along for the ride and of course Annie pays their way. I don't know Annie all that well but from what I observe, her boyfriends are not good matches for her. It is important to note here that they are never dismissed by the kind and generous Annie. They instead become her really good friends.

Some of these single friends have children to whom Annie quickly gets very much attached. She watches these children grow into adulthood and she plans many trips and get togethers for them through the years. She remains friends with the dads and soon becomes friends with their new significant others. Annie is the kind of person who has no enemies.

She has graduated from staying in the smallest least expensive room to a larger room so she can bring kids and also her exes along with her. One year she not only brought two children, but also their dad and his new girlfriend. For some reason the new girlfriend did not like the arrangements so she pouted alone in her car, chain smoking the whole stay. The boyfriend (now the ex to both the lady in the car as well as to Annie) had the whole weekend to spend the way he chose while Annie babysat and entertained his children. Everyone except the now ex girlfriend hibernating in the car had a wonderful time.

I started to keep a list of the guys Annie brought along on her visits but the list grew too long to be helpful. It is fun to see her come through the office door with someone new. I will often say things such as, "Now whom did you bring this year? Which one is this? This is not the same guy you brought last year." She just laughs and introduces him. The one thing these beaus have in common is an instability of some sort as well as no desire to hike or do Annie's favorite things. I know some day she will arrive at the inn with the perfect man for her and I can't wait to see this happen. This perfect couple will have to elope because with all her friends and exes, a wedding ceremony would have way too many guests. This new husband will be very positive, happy, settled, and will love to hike the trails of Acadia with Annie. I know a great place for them to spend their honeymoon!

SPOKES, BIOSTRINGS, AND LINKS

There is an interesting couple and son that have been coming to Seacroft since we opened. I have been keeping tabs on Links since he was just a year old on their first visit in 1993. They would return every year after that, sometimes twice until Links got old enough for school. It was fun watching him grow up as he is the same age as my older granddaughter.

I was racking my brain to think of something I could write about them since they always seemed to take care of themselves. They had been coming to Mt. Desert Island since 1980 way before there was a Seacroft. They knew that the area had great biking routes, free tennis courts, and a variety of golf courses. Their neighboring friends had moved to Bar Harbor to open a wine and cheese shop and loved their new surroundings. Knowing BioStrings' family well they enticed them to make the long haul from their home near Philadelphia for a visit. As I mentioned before, that visit turned into at least one a year since then. I email BioStrings occasionally and mentioned to her that I was writing inn stories and wanted to write their story but I wasn't sure if I could make it as interesting as they are.

The same day I emailed this thought I started receiving

a multitude of emails back from BioStrings with some wonderful suggestions with many of the incidences involving them I had long forgotten. They not only had great memories of their stays but kept discussing the fun they had over the years while getting together at their dining table. Knowing I use pseudonyms they even chose names for themselves that describe their major hobbies and in the case of BioStrings, her career as well. You can guess what those hobbies are.

It is fun to read their emails and to hear what Seacroft has meant to them. They had tried various lodging places around town, a different one every year never quite finding the right fit - that is until they stayed at the newly created Seacroft with their small son and immediately felt at home. I will write about their memories and add a few of my own. Some of this script is in their own words.

On their first visit they rented the apartment. It was attached between the first and second floor with a narrow steep stairway with a head bumper landing. They enjoyed the roominess for the three of them plus their sitter. They were proud to announce that they neither fell down the stairs or bumped their heads. Since the tricky stairway was there for over one hundred years we considered it grandfathered.

They kept renting this big unit until we shut off the stairs at both ends and made two units, a studio with full kitchen, bath, and private deck on the first floor and a two bedroom unit with a mini kitchen upstairs. The threesome then started to rent the upstairs. (A little side note here - The studio has since become a favorite room for a lot of guests. There are repeat customers that try to finagle it for themselves for the nicest times of the season. A Seacroft Policy - If guests take the same room for the same time every year it is automatically theirs the next year.) The roomy two bedroom upstairs is a family favorite and books quickly when kids are out of school for the summer.

BioStrings said they would chuckle discussing the king waterbed that was in one of the bedrooms on the second floor. When we opened Seacroft our tight budget required us to use everything we already owned, anything that was free or cheap. We had the waterbed in our old farmhouse and it made the move to our new room at Seacroft and then on to the apartment. It was fairly easy to move since it was made up of seven tubes one could easily fill from a hose and carry. These tubes of water fit into a boxlike mattress. Guests would be surprised, some delighted and some not, when they discovered they were going to experience a waterbed. BioStrings said she had memories of floating away to sleep and not the nightmares of seasickness from the whaleboat. They considered it a Hoot and it was a sad year when the waterbed went missing.

I emailed back saying I was sorry they missed a Memorial Day event caused by a big leak in the ancient waterbed. Luckily a furniture store nearby was open holidays and immediately delivered a new and more conventional box spring and mattress. The same delivery disposed of the boxlike mattress and seven empty tubes. It really was not that sad for us as we had eked out a long life from our purchase twelve years before. It did create a longer clean up time since there was a great deal of wet bedding and sopping up water just about everywhere in the vicinity of the leaking waterbed. I cannot remember of anyone complaining about that bed but I am pretty sure it was not appreciated by all.

Links remembered the challenge I gave him every year. We were always making small improvements in our guest rooms and it was his job each visit to discover the changes. They might have been a new paint color, a different TV with a DVD player, a comforter, whatever, but he would search until he could report to me these changes. His reward varied over time from Happy Meal toys to a hookless shower curtain the year he went away to Penn State. The family was so proud of him for following in his dad's and granddad's footsteps. That was a sad year for me when Links did not return to Seacroft. I haven't seen him since but I hear he has grown up into a fine young man with a great career and a brand new condo. I have memories of Sue and Rocco or Dave taking him to golf courses when his folks wanted to do their own thing. Of course Links was always the winner.

Speaking of Sue and Rocco, I mentioned that they were on hand to run the inn for the month that we remained in Florida when Dave was seeking treatment for his illness. The two couples got to know each other well and shared their apps, wine, and cheese on the front lawn every afternoon. They remain friends even today and keep in touch. When we arrived home after the long time away from the inn we noticed the four of them on the lawn eating and chatting. They looked disappointed at our return but graciously offered their treats to us. We declined feeling it would have been an interruption of their fun. Even our dog did not seem to be that happy to see us. He had been having a grand time with all his extra attention and treats and had gained a few pounds.

Spokes and BioStrings recommended many acquaintances to stay with us, and some have become regulars, even when the playful couple talked us into short sheeting their beds the day of their arrival. There was a little back and forth of this exercise so I was glad that Kady learned how to do it. I thought her life must have been pretty isolated when I discovered she had no idea what short sheeting was.

BioStrings mentioned many things (and some she said I probably shouldn't mention). The long list includes their shipping ahead bikes and diapers for us to deal with, a broken wine glass, a refrigerator she flubbed up by adjusting it with a broken dial, the laundry situation when I tried to keep Spokes' shorts that looked like Dave's, my keeping her blue ice pack year after year for her, the consulting of Spokes to improve our iffy WIFI, picking up the new Harry Potter books for Links and my granddaughter from that big event at the nearby bookstore, Dave having to reset the TV after little Links kept adjusting the remote, their feeling sorry for Dave who seemed to work very hard while they were having fun, (I wondered if they noticed I worked pretty hard myself), enjoying cable which they didn't have at home, being at Seacroft during the time that Michael Jackson and Tim Russet died and the Aruba girl went missing, the pajama party with most of the other guests on the front deck during the eclipse, the two visits with just rain everyday, the cigars on the deck that are no longer allowed, the time Spokes had his picture taken for the local paper playing tennis with his stogie that was bigger than him, on and on, etc. etc. etc. And to think that I couldn't think of a thing to write about them until I got their emails. It has been twenty-five years since we first met them, and they are still coming. I am glad we are doing something right, and that we appeal to folks like Spokes, BioStrings, and Links.

CHERRY PIE AND SHARK MEAT, FOOD CAN BE FUN - OR NOT

Here we go again with the food. Once in awhile Food can be Fun. At least I try to make it fun. Some of my family was around so I thought we could pick some cherries from our over ripe cherry tree, pit them, and I would make a pie. Well, no one seemed to enjoy my suggestion and I found myself doing everything from the picking to the pitting to the putting the pie together. It was a pretty exhausting project for someone who hated to be in the kitchen for any great length of time. Those cherries were very small and it took a lot of them. They also seemed to be very sour so a lot of sugar was required.

The job was finally finished and the pie baked to a golden brown. The oven was covered with cherry juice, the kitchen was filled with smoke, but the nice scent of baking wafted throughout the inn. I started cutting pie wedges for each member of the family that was hovering around. However, it turned out that no one even liked cherry pie. I ate my small piece and decided it was good enough to give away so started checking with guests to see if there were any takers.

There was a couple from Canada that did not speak much English but they understood what I was saying when I offered them the treat. They had stars in their eyes at the prospect of eating that cherry pie. I happily gave them the whole thing minus my slice, complete with paper plates, napkins, and plastic forks. They raved about the delicious pie and my willingness to gift such a prize. They even picked their own cherries and packed them up for the trip home.

They returned to Canada and told friends all about it. I henceforth called them the Cherry Pie People and they called themselves the same in a thick French accent whenever they called for a reservation. I saw them often as well as their friends who came to the inn. Their friends would introduce themselves as friends of the Cherry Pie People. Over the years I have seen this couple return many times and each time we chuckled about that Cherry Pie. The last time I saw them they were dressed to the nines, had stopped smoking, and had taken English lessons. They showed a new confidence about themselves. This big change I witnessed in them had nothing to do with the Cherry Pie and it did not change the major topic of our talks. They spoke very good English and our conversations continued to be mostly about that pie.

One of the things guests like to do when they come to the island is to go deep sea fishing. The problem with that arises when they catch something, and don't know what they should do with it. Our in room freezers aren't big enough to preserve their fish and our kitchens just have microwaves for cooking. So one time we, who are not fish eaters, were gifted with some shark meat. I asked my friends and neighbors if they wanted it and there were no takers. So I thought I would expand the gustatory experiences of my guests by cooking and offering each one a sample of shark meat.

To my despair there were again no takers, not even to taste the small samples I offered. I honestly thought these guests would go home and enjoy bragging that they got to taste shark. So much for my great food ideas. The shark meat samples were tossed into the trash.

To stay on the subject of fun or lack of it where food is concerned I would like to describe my Breakfast Baskets. As I have mentioned I do not like to cook or bake so have devised a plan to keep it to a minimum. We have a great set up to promote this with restaurants around every corner just a short walk away from the inn. We also have mini kitchens with microwaves, toasters, coffeepots, dishes, and small refrigerators in our rooms. Regular guests know the set up and take care of their own breakfasts. New guests or late arrivals often want the breakfast basket brought to their rooms for convenience more than anything.

I purchased clam baskets and lined them with homemade cloth napkins. The basket basics are made up of paper and plastic products and four items; Fruit, Juice, Pastry (homemade muffin or bagel or popover), and Yogurt or Granola Bar. I don't take requests but I do ask about allergies. I am not a short order cook but I don't want to kill anyone either. When a child under 12 is part of the party I add a toy of some sort that makes it fun for the child. One of my young guests keeps me supplied with Happy Meal Toys that are great for certain ages. Thank you, Jake.

Breakfasts are not included in the rate. If anyone requests it there is a $5 charge for each person so the price is right. There are times I don't have to bake a muffin for two weeks and there are times when I have to make three batches a day for a week. All considered it is pretty easy. I am always looking for the easiest solutions, especially where food is concerned. Food preparation is what I like the least about my inn business so I keep it to a minimum but I always attempt to make it fun.

KNOWN BEST BY THEIR NICKNAMES

I have already mentioned the Cherry Pie people from Canada but other folks are also referred to and remembered mostly by their nicknames. I mean no disrespect by using these nicknames because I really like these people. Three couples come to mind: the Tide People, The Mushroom People, and the Karaoke Couple. We all have good and not so good habits and these people are no different. They have all stayed for many visits for many years and then moved on to do other things.

The retired Doctor and his wife would stay a week at a time and they always requested the same room a year in advance. He would spend the whole day in Acadia, hiking, biking, and photographing. She was a nester rarely leaving her room. I remember that she read, painted, and apparently complained a lot to her husband but never to me. She had allergies that made her feel ill and she complained to him about the detergent I used. After the first visit, the doctor would call ahead of time and request that I launder everything in the room with regular Tide just like they used at home with success.

Before their first day I would religiously launder everything washable from their room: the linens, mattress cover, pillow covers, blankets, comforter, towels, tub mat, dish cloths, shower curtain, etc. in regular Tide. This was not my regular detergent and it was all very time consuming and I believe unnecessary. She would have a bad night and he would come in the next morning to tell me she couldn't sleep because she was allergic to something in the room. I told him I had done as he had asked but I witnessed him loading up all the bedding and taking it to the Laundromat with his jug of Tide.

On one visit he presented me with what he thought was a Glade scented plug-in that was in their outlet. It was a rodent deterrent that caused vibrations intended to discourage little creatures from sharing their space. It had no scent whatsoever. She also said she had food allergies so could only eat certain things so I strongly suggested she supply her own breakfasts and snacks since I could not please her with my choices. The doc just wanted her happy so he could leave for the day and do his own thing. I think she was happy because she had been successful in constantly pulling his chain. At least that was my interpretation from my observation.

The Mushroom People outnumber all the rest. They are the ones that love air conditioning no matter what the weather is. Many rentals in Bar Harbor do not have air conditioning because frankly there are very few days that it is needed. We tried convincing people all they had to do was to open their windows to get the ocean breeze. There are probably just a very few days when the temps get over 80 degrees, and we personally enjoy having our windows open day and night. We have no a.c. units in our private quarters. We, however, began to realize we lost a lot of business especially from southern states with high humidity such as Florida, the Carolinas, and Virginia. These folks hang indoors in air conditioned homes as much as possible in the summer. They do not plan to vacation anywhere that doesn't have a.c. even in Maine near the ocean.

We relented for the sake of improving our business and put window units in the warmest rooms that got the most sun. Shortly after that we installed nice units in all the rooms. The rooms previously heated with central heat now have heaters in the same units. These work out well because people like to have that control, the ability to determine the temperature in their rooms. There are times when every a.c. unit is running and the temps are in the 70's or cooler. I have to admit that this bothers me to the core. I think it is a waste and I am paying the bill for it.

When we enter rooms just vacated to clean them we find them cold, damp, and extremely stuffy. The first thing we do is to turn off the a.c.s and open the windows. New guests enter their clean, fresh rooms with the windows open and an ocean breeze wafting through them. Some guests appreciate this but others do not. Often the first thing on their agenda is to close the windows and turn on the a.c.s I realize a small percentage of folks rely on a.c.s to improve their health conditions, such as ringing ears and allergies. I am glad to have the units for people who really need them. And for those few extremely warm days with high humidity it is nice to have them for everyone. Guests that have their air conditioners running day and night are affectionately called Mushroom People because like mushrooms they love cool damp places.

I remember well the time a man was checking out a room to see if it was suitable for a night's stay for him and his wife. It was early in our inn days when we were trying out a few window units. This potential guest asked Dave if that small unit would cool off that big room. Dave said in his good Maine accent and without hesitation, "Not as well as opening the windows."

The Karaoke Couple was a bit different. I think the singing was a new hobby for them. We have had many really good musicians that practice instruments while here, but I do not recall anyone singing to recorded music. This couple was clearly having a great time singing at the top of their lungs with the windows wide open. They had come for years and the thing they loved to do the most was not the singing but the cooking and dining on lobsters daily. Another nickname that fits almost every guest is Lobster Lover. There are just too many of them so we have never used that nickname. This couple and many others pretty well finished off the old apartment- sized range. The burners were going or gone and the drip pans were full and overflowing with foul smelling lobster water often. It was time to get a new stove. It was the only room with a stove and it had caused multiple problems in the past. It took precious time to clean the oven, stovetop, and pots and pans. A few of our guests were clearly into cooking their own meals. I remember too many bacon and fishy smells permeating the whole building and I did not want that kind of inn. I decided it was time to just eliminate the stove all together. Our guests would have to do with just the microwave. When the Karaoke Couple came to the office to reserve for the next year I told them I was eliminating the stove. I could tell by their unhappy expressions that they had completed their last stay at Seacroft. I do like the stove gone, but I do miss this nice couple very much. I see them around town so I am sure they are still singing and cooking lobster in their new digs.

BABESIOSIS AND BUD

Babesiosis is a tick borne disease that affects some people seriously and others with no symptoms at all. These ticks are hardly ever noticed by their victims because they are about the size of poppy seeds. Malaria and flu like symptoms can be deadly serious and very difficult to diagnose. When Bud and Lil showed up for their annual visit, Bud did not look like himself. He gave me the usual hug and curiously left his head resting on my shoulder. I think I was momentarily holding him upright. He felt very warm and I knew he had a high temperature. Lil ushered him quickly up to the second floor to the room they always reserve. She said he had a urinary tract infection and had not been feeling well.

When the ambulance arrived in front of the inn a couple of hours later I knew where to go. Lil had tried to get Bud to rest but he was insistent on taking a shower and going out to eat to celebrate their anniversary. While exiting the tub he felt light headed and fell to the bathroom floor. Lil could not get him up and he seemed to be incoherent. She called an ambulance immediately. When I got to their room the paramedics were trying to get his consent to go to the hospital. Bud was not having any of that and refused. He just wanted to go to bed. The paramedics told Lil they needed his permission to transport him to the hospital

Lil is a retired nurse and knew he had to get treatment. As I was observing and wondering how I could help, I witnessed Lil using her firm nurse's tone. Being a woman of small stature she had to tip her head way back to see the face of a very tall paramedic. She demanded in no uncertain terms that they take Bud to the hospital. His temperature had shot way up and she knew he was very ill. The paramedics quickly decided they should do what she asked. She had things well in hand and off they all went in the ambulance.

Bud got tests and treatment for his high temperature. Results showed he needed surgery on his gall bladder. He was so ill they did not want to operate in our small hospital so they transported him to Bangor. They reviewed the test results there and luckily had witnessed these same symptoms in other patients earlier in the season. Bud had been infected by the Babesiosis tick and his red blood cells were infected and compromised. He was seriously ill. He did not need surgery but he was in need of medication immediately. They kept him in the hospital for over a week until Bud could stand the long trip back home to PA. His son is a physician and worked with the medical staff both long distance and also at the hospital.

On his way north Bud had come through Connecticut that is famous for ticks, but the incubation period made them think this tick did its dirty deed at his PA home while he was doing yard work. It was months before Bud felt well enough to get back to some of his daily activities. About three months later Bud gave me a call and let me know he was on the mend. He described how ill he had been and he said he came close to death. He still felt weak and had lost a lot of weight but for the first time was beginning to feel like himself.

I had my doubts that they would return the following

year but they did. It was so nice to see this couple the way they always had appeared before The Tick Incident. Bud and Lil did their favorite things and were joined by their daughter and grandchildren. I think this wonderful couple always enjoyed life but somehow they seem to appreciate it even more now after that terrible scare.

SEWER IN THE CELLAR

Relatives were visiting and were willing to help out and that is a good thing. Sue and Rocco are great cooks and are always offering to take over the kitchen, which as you know is good news for me. But something else was unfolding at the inn at that time and it was beginning to smell. The main sewer exit was partially plugged. The good thing here is the word, partial. Most of the sewer was exiting like it should when the contents were gradual. However around 9 am when a dozen toilets were flushing and showers were running all at the same time, the partial plug did not allow for it all to escape. Luckily the backup was totally in the cellar under our living room, lucky because there was no back up in our guest rooms or our private rooms, lucky because most of the smell was in our private quarters. Our guests did not even realize what was happening.

We called a plumber who came immediately since I told him it was an emergency. The town water company was also on hand since they had the camera that should show us exactly where the problem was. The camera went into what we thought was the sewer exit in the back of the basement but it turned out to be dry and deserted. It is always difficult to work in an older home and there are always searches underway to find the illusive necessities that need fixing. The plumber found a newer exit in the front of the basement. We should have known this since this is where we had the morning floods around the time that 15 to 20 people were getting ready for their day.

These floods were gruesome to look at since they contained raw sewerage and it all smelled fierce. The liquid part would eventually drain out but there was a large amount of solid material left in little piles around the cellar floor that we had to shovel into contractor bags. The plumber said he could fix the problem but we should probably wait until the end of the season as it was time consuming and he would have to turn the water off to the whole inn. He suggested a temporary fix, a company with a powerful pressure hose to blow out the line. We used this system twice to finish out the season.

When the last guest had gone the plumber came back and did a permanent fix on the sewer exit. We determined that the pipe had been cracked years ago when Dave and the carpenter that was working here at the time put in a sump pump. They pounded a hole through the cement floor near the sewer exit. This probably caused a small crack that got larger over the years and eventually allowed sand to seep in and partially plug the pipe.

Sue and Rocco happened to be visiting at the time this was all happening. Rocco would fortify himself and help me shovel the sludge every morning. I saw him walking up the street one morning and asked where he was going. He said, I don't mind helping you shovel Sh__, but I will be darn if I shovel my own. He was headed to the nearest public restroom. At the same time Sue was washing veggies for the day's meals under the outside spigot. These two are a comical pair and willing to do what needs to get done.

They are always the first ones to volunteer when we need help. A different time they were here an elderly guest asked if we would have our porter carry her bags to her room on the second floor. Usually Kady and I manage to come up with a way to take care of this when guests cannot do it for themselves. This time we had a porter, Rocco. He looked at the trunk size suitcase and grunted and groaned his way up the stairs to her room. He said he had never been called a porter before and in nearly 30 years we had never been asked for one. Our porter had departed before the lady with the trunk so it was up to Kady and me to get it back down the stairs and into her car. We had gravity to help and even though some might call us weak old ladies we can usually do almost anything together.

Sue and Rocco were an immense help those sewer days as they always are when they come. They were the relatives that freed up their schedule to completely run the inn when Dave had surgery and we were tied up in Florida for 4 weeks. We will always be eternally grateful for all their assistance.

There were huge bags of sludge left in the cellar that represented the last evidence of the sewer disaster. It took several helpers to get them out of the cellar and into the back of my van. They honestly looked like dead bodies and were about the same weight. Only gravity was at the dump to help me get them from the van. When I was driving away a dump manager walked by the bags with the idea of slinging them into the dumpster with one hand. On the first try the weight of the bag nearly took him to the ground. He was looking at them and scratching his head as I drove by. I was hoping he did not see my license plate. A lot of things are simply not accepted at our transfer station. I knew better than to ask permission to dump this particular material.

AND OTHER TALES FROM THE INN

FRIENDS, FAMILY, AND MISCELLANEOUS TALES

ROD, ONE OF THE GOOD ONES

THE OTHER GOOD ONES

KADY AND THE DIVORCE KAYAK

LINCOLN, A NOT SO GOOD INN DOG

TUCKER, THE PERFECT INN DOG

TABBIE AND THE CAT ROOM

IT SEEMS TO BE THE THING TO DO

BAR BAR BLACK SHEEP

MOM MAKES FRIENDS WHEREVER SHE GOES

VISITORS OTHER THAN THE HUMAN KIND

SEACROFT LAUNDRY SERVICE

INKEEPING 101

WHY I WEAR CLOTHES TO BED

PET PEEVES

THE PROS AND CONS OF A HOME AND
BUSINESS COMBINED

THEN AND NOW

ROD, ONE OF THE GOOD ONES

In 1964, Dave and I graduated from the University of Maine and we were lucky enough for him to land a job at Bar Harbor High School. I always said he majored in Football and Bridge and minored in Math and Science, and he excelled in all of them. Teaching math and coaching football was a dream come true. The high school was small with good teachers who became friends. I did not apply for a job since I was pregnant with our first child, Tracy, who was born in November. I did some substituting and study hall duty and walked constantly to stay fit. I got to know our new town and immediately knew it was something special even in the solitude of winter.

The football games were a big deal in this small town and many fans supported Coach Brown and the Seasiders. Some of the players would often visit our small apartment to talk football and to empty our refrigerator. There were two brothers that I remember well even though it had been well over fifty years. The older one was a handsome gifted athlete who quarterbacked the team. He was destined to have a stellar future. His little brother was less outgoing and didn't make much of a splash as an athlete. Dave spent a lot of time with his players, especially the ones whose dads were very busy with important jobs. The older brother went off to premed school to follow in his dad's footsteps. About that same time we left Bar Harbor for greener pastures in the education field, Rod, the younger brother, was still in high school. He later became a skilled golfer and was close to making it as a pro. After college he came back to the island to start a business and raise a family.

It had been many years since Dave coached football and one of the strict rules for the team back then was NO SMOKING. Rod did not smoke in high school but picked up the habit in adulthood. When Dave and Rod spotted each other around town they would always stop for a chat. Rod was always hopeful that Coach had not seen his cigarette, but of course he always did. The first time this happened Rod hid his lit cigarette behind his back the whole time they were talking. There was a little telltale swirl of smoke rising up behind Rod's head. Dave would keep him talking until the cigarette burned down too far to hold. Rod knew he had been outsmarted. To Rod Dave would always be Coach and the Coach had rules. He couldn't give up the beast but he still felt guilty many years later when the Coach caught him red handed with the lit cigarette.

After returning to Bar Harbor in 1990, we hired Rod to plow out Seacroft. After Dave passed away I hired him and his crew to mow. When we moved to Florida winters he became our inn caretaker also. This is when I really got to know him. He always called me Mrs. Coach. My bills would come every month with a handwritten note to Mrs. Coach. There is not a nicer man that ever lived, but unfortunately he did not live long past his sixty-six birthday. He had suffered a heart attack while attending church.

I have great memories of him in his signature rumpled hat riding around in his truck with his son. He was always checking up on his crew and the work they were doing. The crew told me many times that they were told they had better do a good job for Mrs. Coach. He worked hard to do his job right always wanting to please me. He told me many times how much Dave meant to him.

Rod's older brother ended up with the same cancer that Dave had. He had become a very successful physician in the Portland area. Rod made sure the two of them got together to encourage and to learn from each other. He would come to the inn with his brother and just sit and listen to the two men he respected so much.

Life is sometimes very hard on the really good souls. Rod lost his young daughter, his older brother, a nephew, and his parents all within a very short span. He was not in good health himself often suffering from severe pain, but he always had a big smile when he saw me.

I wanted to mention Rod here since he was the first person we hired when we moved back to Bar Harbor and purchased the inn. We never had to look for a replacement. I cannot say that about any other repair or service personnel. It often took a long time to find the competence level that we expected. I can say now after nearly thirty years that I have found a dependable group of skilled men. I am sad to have to replace the very first man we hired, a wonderful person who always did his job well. He was a trusted friend and I miss him.

THE OTHER GOOD ONES

Rod was a good one and his replacement is working out well. Ken lives just down the road and can plow, care take, and mow. I was lucky to have found someone that really wanted the job and can do all the helpful services that Rod did for us. This is his first year so it is a trial run, but I have a good feeling about him.

After a few years of trying out different companies to do repairs here and there I am satisfied with what I now consider regulars, not guests but repair personnel. With a building over 125 years old, we need good help keeping things up to snuff for our guests. As good as they are there is one company I consider the best of the worst because things still seem to fail at times after being repaired. But they fail less than with the other companies we have tried. The best of the worst is the best I can do. I know because I have tried them all. The key to success with any company is to line up a service in advance and request the technician that has helped the most in the past. I have a list of skilled repairmen that I respect and I always request them when I can.

Beau is an electrician from a reputable company on the island. His daughter is the same age as my granddaughter so we compare stories, pictures, and videos. Then he gets to work. Since he is the one that comes most often and the one I request he knows the secrets that are hiding in the walls and he knows where all eight circuit breaker boxes are. Knowing a lot about Seacroft means he does not have to start from scratch every time there is a problem. He has repaired the simple stuff and in the process found a very dangerous situation with an improperly installed propane fireplace that could have caused a serious fire.

He installed a generator after a major power failure in town on the busy 4th of July weekend that brought forth cold shower complaints. He also installed 26 up-to-date smoke and carbon dioxide detectors recommended by the town fire marshal. These were time consuming jobs but Beau could do them in half the time of newbies because he had gotten to know Seacroft well.

Eddie is a skilled heating and plumbing guy. He can look at the furnace and in less than a minute he knows what is wrong with it, what has to be replaced, and what parts he needs. He is the one that discovered where and why our sewer backed up into the cellar; he suggested a temporary repair to get us to the end of the season, and then came back to permanently repair the problem. He is the only furnace guy that has done the fall maintenance that made the furnace happy enough to make it through the winter. It also turns out that he is a licensed propane technician so he will be useful when I get the new propane furnace. I, of course, always ask for Eddie.

There is a paint crew new to me that does excellent work and they all seem comfortable on three story ladders. Most painters refuse the job after they see the high gables with wood trim. The owner of the painting company, Buck, fell in love with Seacroft while working here and made a reservation to bring his wife for a weekend getaway (she needed to get away from their four small children for a short while). He also did a small job free of charge long after his crews were done and gone. Kady had painted a hallway with a high ceiling and couldn't quite reach the tops of the walls. One of the painters came back with a sixteen foot ladder. After he finished the job he said he was not supposed to charge anything.

And then there is Ryan, a finished carpenter who does jobs big and small. I give him what we call simply, THE LIST, in the fall. We walk through the inn, up and down stairs to cellar and attic, and go through the different items on THE LIST. He carefully makes notes in a small orange notebook and takes pictures. I hear from him occasionally during the winter if he has a question or notices something out of place at the inn. I get an email bill carefully itemized with each item he purchased, the number of hours he worked, and pictures of the finished projects. I feel really accomplished as I sit by my Florida pool. The inn projects are finished, I know what they look like, and I am not even there.

Ryan carefully listens to what I want because he respects me. Believe me this is not always the case because a lot of men think they know a lot more than this old lady. I surmise this when they half listen and roll their eyes. They just want to get something done so they can leave. Ryan wants to make sure the end product is what I want. I often say, "Do it the way you would like it done." I have never been disappointed.

Often guests mention some of his projects and wish they had a Ryan around to help them. He built a small shed to hold the trash and recycle bins. Often wannabe do it yourselfers check it out and admire the craftsmanship. Critters of the night cannot get in to strew debris around the yard and it isn't because of Ryan's sign, "Raccoons - Keep Out!"

One year his job was to rebuild the large side deck that was showing signs of rot. He first had to redo the underpinning, and then he could lay the decking boards. He put off that chore for a while because he knew the boards would not look right on the ends. The width of the deck varied so some of the boards would end in a point and that would not look good.

His wife picked him up that day and he told her about his problem. She quickly suggested he put the boards at an angle. He was elated because this was such a simple solution. It was so different that he emailed me to get my okay. I thought it was a great idea and suggested a 90 degree angle off the patio door which was offset at a 45 degree angle to the deck. "The perfect solution," he said. He laid the boards taking the time to scroll around the original granite posts. He also used clamps to secure the boards so the screws would not show. The finished product is very unique and very professionally done. Ryan knows that women often have great ideas.

If there is something that needs to be changed and I am not sure how, we talk about it and come up with a plan. I needed some way to keep a bathroom door from closing. The door would shut itself when anyone came out. We never knew if someone was in there, and the other problem was that the heat could not enter the room. I kept a rock there to brace it but I was the only one that seemed to use it. I was always finding the door closed. Ryan installed a reversed door closer that opens it quickly and efficiently with a clunk. It always surprises first time users and it is a pretty humorous system. It usually gets further investigation and I often hear a chuckle after the clunk.

When a 90-year-old friend of mine broke her pelvis she found herself unable to use her stairs when she got out of the hospital. Ryan dropped everything and installed a special railing that allowed her to go upstairs where her bedroom and bath were. He has since made her a downstairs bathroom and done other jobs around her home. Ryan does everything well and I don't know what I would do without his expertise. It was a lucky find when I saw him working at my neighbors' summer home several years ago. I hired him on the spot. Thank you, Ryan. Every home and business owner would be lucky to have a Rod, a Ken, a Beau, an Eddie, a Buck, and a Ryan. They all work hard to keep my inn humming.

KADY AND THE DIVORCE KAYAK

Kayaking was a favorite sport for both Dave and me. We bought some second hand kayaks the first year we moved to town. They were old school, very inefficient, but also very stable. We could take them for short trips, perhaps two hours, which was our limit, since we would stiffen up in the sitting position, feet straight out in front of us, and paddling constantly. When we had a time window away from the inn we would head toward one of the islands and either circle around it or beach our watercrafts and do a little beachcombing.

Lobstermen would be pulling traps all around us. Sometimes we would circle the big cruise ships anchored in the harbor. That was before 9/11. After the terrorist attack we were not allowed to go near them. There were small Coast Guard boats on alert all around them. The QEII was a particularly pretty old ship with a massive pointed hull. The newer huge ships seem square and lacking of character. There is a hierarchy of boats. Kayaks are speed bumps to lobster boats, and lobster boats are speed bumps to cruise ships.

A long time ago a single lady guest asked me if I would take her out for a paddle so I did. Candy said she had lots of experience in canoes and kayaks. Let's just say you can't believe everything one says. There were no waves that day but the wind was blowing like it often does on the ocean. We got started by Balance Rock and headed out to the breakwater. I intended to stay very close to shore and inside the breakwater. I noticed the wind had picked up even more and was blowing us away from shore. I told Candy we needed to turn back and try again another time. She was struggling and I realized she didn't have the strength or knowhow to turn against the wind. She started screaming my name. I tried to talk to her but she couldn't hear me. The wind was carrying her out to sea. I quickly headed back to shore and kept my eye on her red jacket.

I needed to get help to rescue her so beached my kayak on the rocks on the Shore Path and ran to the Town Wharf where the Harbor Master was. I could see her red jacket near one of the Porcupines so the Harbor Master and I set out in his boat to retrieve her and my kayak. After we safely returned to the wharf he started to scold her. I stopped him and said it was my entire fault for going out on a windy day. Candy and I collected both kayaks and got them back to Seacroft. It was really unreal how calm it was on land compared to just a few yards off shore.

I, of course, apologized to Candy for causing her such a frightening experience. I praised her for keeping her head and for paddling to stay inside the Porcupines. We laughed about the possibility of her ending up in Europe the way the wind was blowing that day. I am not sure if she or I was more scared. I have never taken another guest out in a kayak and I don't recall Candy ever returning to Seacroft.

Recently Kady asked if we could go kayaking. It was something she had always wanted to do. It was a quiet day at the inn, it was warm and sunny, and there was no wind. Kady was not a guest but was and still is my entire staff. I know her well. She is a quick learner and possesses a great deal of common sense. We hauled the kayaks down Albert Meadow to Balance Rock at high tide and started paddling. We stayed near shore, looked for sea stars at the breakwater, chatted, and had a fun time. Someone took our picture so she had proof of her adventure to show her family when she returned to Florida for the winter.

The second time we went paddling we went to a Chamber function that was sponsored by a lakeside canoe and kayak rental business. Chamber members that own tourist businesses such as this will give other chamber members the chance to experience what they offer. We in turn are in a good position to promote it to our customers. When we first moved to Bar Harbor and opened the inn we went to practically every restaurant for a free meal as well as on whale watches, nature and lighthouse tours, bus tours, scenic flights, to improv and dinner theaters, and to other assorted offerings. Some newer businesses in town are standup paddle boarding which I would love to try and rock climbing which I had just as soon leave to someone else. We don't go as much now to these free functions but the chance to kayak on Long Pond and then after be served refreshments were both very enticing. Shortly after arriving we were given a tandem kayak, lifejackets, and paddles. We took off and headed toward the nearby water lilies and loon families.

Kady was having a lot of fun but I was struggling and cursing. The paddles didn't have drip rings so I was getting soaked from water running down the paddle. The tandem did not have a rudder so I couldn't steer the thing. We were zigzagging the whole way. I kept telling Kady to do this and stop doing that until she told me to stop being a backseat driver. I think she really told me to Shut Up. We got tired and wet very fast so did not end up going very far. When we got back to shore the young man collecting our equipment took one look at us and started chuckling. He said, "You gals got the Divorce Kayak." It was nice to know that we were not the only ones that came back very unhappy with that particular kayak. The fun part of our trip was getting to know the loons, hearing their calls, and watching the babies riding on their moms' backs. So long loons and hello hamburgers. We had worked up an appetite and it was nice of the owners to feed us so well. I just hope they got rid of that darn kayak.

Some folks load their kayaks onto their car racks and travel great distances for their paddling trips. We just enjoy pulling them down the street on dollies. We learned it is smart to put in and take out our kayaks close to high tide. At a low tide we have to drag our boats over the seaweed for quite a distance and it can be dangerously slippery and time consuming.

Each Island in the Porcupines has it own charm. Bar Island has a bar at low tide and many tourists and locals like to walk to the island, hike the trails there, and watch for wildlife. Some tourists not accustomed to tides will park their cars on the bar. This is allowed but not very smart. They take nice long hikes returning too late to reach their car that is on its way to getting submerged. These folks need rescuing by a local boat owner and now there is a fee for this service. The vehicle is not so lucky.

During the Prohibition era liquor was often smuggled into Bar Harbor and left on one of the islands. One even became known as Rum Island. Sheep Island has a nice beach where you can pull up and explore. For years the Blue Nose Ferry would chug between Sheep and Burnt Islands on its way to Canada and back making daily trips during the summer season. The original Blue Nose was eventually replaced by a high-speed catamaran that could make the trip in 3 hours. This no longer exists. Now anyone wanting to go to Nova Scotia from Bar Harbor has to drive the 700 miles.

I love the unique beauty of Long Island. It has a narrow canyon that you can paddle into with tall sides and loud echoes. It is too narrow to turn around in so one has to back out. There are also beachy areas where many people have their lobster bakes. Bald Island is on the end of the breakwater and has sheer cliffs on the side of the open ocean. One can watch birds floating on the swells and it is a great feeling to allow your kayak to ride those swells with the birds. In the spring the islands are alive with baby seals. Often dolphins will swim beside your kayak and socialize. When they come up for air they sound human. You often see eagles and ospreys and their nests at the tops of trees.

Kayaking is a fun sport in so many ways. One has to be respectful of the power of the ocean and use common sense. Many kayakers have lost their lives being careless and taking too many chances. It is best to get to know the sport by going in groups and with a guide. When the amateurs ask about capsizing, the guides used to say, "No one has ever tipped a kayak over on our trips." For some reason they no longer say that. There are classes in kayak safety. We learned what equipment we should have on us as well as how to get back into an overturned kayak. It was only then that we started our kayaking adventures. Other than my close call with Candy we have never had a problem. Candy and I were lucky she lived to see another day. That whole adventure was a huge mistake on my part and I learned a great deal from it.

LINCOLN, A NOT SO GOOD INN DOG

We have had dogs during our years of running the inn. All of us are partial to Cocker Spaniels, and they were all great inn dogs. Tucker was the last one to share our home, but more about him and his special personality later.

My Brooklyn daughter, Tammy, likes to get out of the sweltering city with her family in the summer. Her job allows her some time off, and she can handle most situations by computer. One of her family members that she adored was a big rescue mutt she named Lincoln. As a pup he was tiny with small paws and he was marked like a Boston terrier. They thought a small dog would be a wonderful addition to their family that at the time consisted of a busy couple with careers. Lincoln always thought Tammy was his mother and they were inseparable. Lincoln grew and grew until he was close to one hundred pounds. He had long gangly legs making him look like a greyhound but he was closer in size to a Great Dane.

He showed signs of being intelligent so Tammy taught him all sorts of tricks. She was anxious for him to get out of the city in the summer also. He would sleep in the back of their car most of the trip, but as they approached the bridge that leads to our island, he would snap awake and

99

start sniffing the ocean air. Oh, Boy. He remembered this was a good thing.

Tammy would walk him mornings and his favorite place was the beach. He had this trick where he would find a rock the right size and hike it just like a football center. People would watch him and laugh at his antics. If Tammy dared take him off leash he would play keep away (from her) when it was time to leave. This also got plenty of laughs from the standbys. Tammy didn't think it was all that funny.

Lincoln was harmless but had a streak where he would charge large dogs probably thinking he should be protecting his mother. He had a very loud bark that jarred the neighbors in the old warehouse apartment building where he lived in Brooklyn. He also used that loud bark at the inn and I didn't appreciate it. I always have the customers in mind and want them to have a great experience. Loud barking isn't one of them.

If there were two people present when the doorbell rang, the nearest one would grab his collar. He knew this meant he might as well be quiet. If there were only one person there he was in his glory. He would rush the door, barking viciously, and scaring some guests out of their shoes. Even if I had a choking grip on his collar he would continue to bark the whole check in time.

One day a man came to the door with the look of someone that had been tasered. He asked questions about the inn. He had been awake all night and was looking for a quiet place to stay, preferably that did not allow pets. The inn where he was staying had several visiting dogs that had barked day and night. Paying nearly $400 a night had not guaranteed this poor man a quiet room. Lincoln was upstairs in the den with Tammy who was working on the computer. He got wind that somebody new was at the door. He came rushing down the spiral staircase and charged the man with his angry sounding bark.

There was nothing I could say as I grabbed at Lincoln's

collar. The man looked completely defeated, turned around, and went back out the door. I knew he would never return. This might not have been the only time Lincoln had cost us a customer.

Lincoln also nearly caused our plumber to have a heart attack. George was a pretty good plumber and heating specialist and was one of the repairmen that came to the inn regularly. On one of his visits he was climbing the narrow spiral staircase from the cellar to the kitchen to check on a dripping faucet. He was a bit overweight and was slowed down on his ascent by rubbing heavily on both sides of the railings. He thought about turning around and going out the bulkhead to the front door but couldn't physically do that so he just kept climbing.

Upon opening the door to the kitchen he was met face to face with Lincoln. I am not sure who was more frightened, the plumber who was wedged at the top of the staircase and couldn't move backwards or the trembling Great Dane sized marshmallow that was trying to do his duty as a protector.

Now Lincoln wouldn't hurt a soul but he had the loudest and scariest bark you could imagine. The standoff seemed to take forever and I couldn't help since I was on the spiral staircase behind the plumber. I did try to convince George that he was not in any danger but I don't think he believed me. Someone from the upstairs area finally came to the rescue and calmed Lincoln so the shaking plumber could move forward into the kitchen. Lincoln continued staring down the plumber with a low-grade growl as he moved about fixing the faucet. It was actually pretty comical to us but maybe not to George.

I have since asked several repairmen from the same company if they heard the story of George getting stopped at the top of the cellar stairs by the very large and very loud guard dog. They all seemed to have heard the story from George himself who for some reason has never returned to Seacroft.

WHY I WEAR CLOTHES TO BED

Lincoln has since passed away and we all miss him dearly. He had a pampered life and like most dogs brought much joy to the lives around him. Even now when Tammy and her family are at the inn summers and the doorbell rings, we all jump and get ready to grab Lincoln's collar. Tammy now brings my adorable granddaughter that has helped to fill the void and adds a whole new dimension to all of our lives. She is a lively one and bears watching but we don't have to worry about her scaring the guests like her predecessor. The people on the beach now watch a cute little girl making sand castles instead of the comical mutt who liked to hike rocks.

TUCKER, THE PERFECT INN DOG

Tucker came to us as a puppy. We were not really looking for a pet since we were so busy at the time. A friend, Walt, knew that we were cocker spaniel lovers and had lost our pets recently. He came to us bearing a gift, the cutest puppy you could imagine. We welcomed them both and the puppy's father who was also with them. Rascal was a beautiful stud cocker that had a sweet nature. His son, Twister, would someday look just like him but he was better behaved than his dad when it came to food. More about that a little later. Twister definitely entertained us for the next few minutes as he ventured away from his father to the Christmas tree on the sun porch. He poked around the wrapped packages and came away with a ribbon stuck to his nose. He was very proud of himself for that maneuver. I knew right then he would be staying at our home.

With the ribbon still on his nose he went back to follow his father around. While Twister had been under the tree Rascal had found a tuna sandwich just waiting to be grabbed. He shared a little of it with Twister and they both soon smelled like fish. Twister grabbed Rascal's tuna covered ear and was dragged back to where we were watching the events. It was obvious that both father and son were extremely good natured and had adorable personalities. Walt and Rascal left the inn and Twister stayed behind with us for the next eleven years. He never missed a beat and loved us all from the beginning. Even though he was not used to sleeping without his mother in a dog crate he did not whimper all night. He was part of our family from the minute he pranced into our lives.

One of the recent pets we had lost was a lovable but rather dumb cocker named Bucky. We wanted to name our new family member a combination of Bucky and Twister so came up with Tucker which fit him to a tee. He quickly responded to the new name. He also quickly learned every trick we could think of. With a few NO commands he never stole food even within easy reach. He would guard it for you if you had to leave it on the coffee table for fifteen minutes or more. I am sure he would never let another dog take it, but he would never take it himself.

We all took walks with Tucker on the Carriage Roads in the park. He would always be on guard for us pointing out everything that looked different than the day before. One time he suddenly stopped and was obviously spooked. He did not want us to keep going. We had seen signs of coy dogs in the area and I believe he knew they were around or had been around. He was very happy when we turned around and headed back to our car.

If Tucker saw a flock of egrets in a field in Florida or a deer or two on the Acadia Carriage Roads, he would watch with wonder. If the creatures were close up he was conflicted. He pretended not to see them because he wasn't sure what he should do. If they flew or ran away he would take off bravely chasing them. Once he pulled the leash out of Dave's hand and took off through the woods, Dave hightailing it after him. If his leash had not gotten caught up on a stump he would still be running after that deer.

He once saved me from a serious injury or death. I tripped taking him down a steep bank to his favorite brook, and I could not get my footing. As I was flying downhill rapidly I kept grabbing at bushes and limbs to slow myself down. Tucker luckily went on the other side of a tree and he and the leash finally stopped my descent.

On another walk near town he slowed his pace and started to proceed with caution. His eyes were glued to something far up ahead of us. I could not tell what it was until we got closer. I could smell fresh paint and noticed that a fire hydrant had just been painted. He had sensed that something was different about it and had warned us to be careful about the change.

He loved walking into a cool stream on hot days and he knew where they all were. He would go into a trance it felt so good to him. He would take a long drink and not come out until we forced him to. One time he inadvertently got in over his head. It scared him and he never went near that particular spot again. He never liked our Florida pool either. We tried to coax him in but he would have nothing to do with it. As a puppy he tried to walk across the pool blanket and must have fallen in because he came to me all wet. I was on the phone and was not watching him but luckily he saved himself. I went to the pool to see if I could see what had happened. His favorite toy was sitting on the blanket in the middle of the pool. He had tried to rescue it and could easily have drowned. After that I never stopped watching him when he went near that scary pool.

He quickly adjusted to our routine of spending summers in Bar Harbor and winters in Cape Coral. Both places had his toys and dishes and he would go directly to them when he entered his homes. He loved toys, particularly stuffed animals. He liked new ones that he would grab and maim. After this particular exercise he would usually discard them never to play with them again. One day I brought bags full of groceries back to the inn and had to take care of a guest that had arrived at the same time. I put the bags on the floor. Tucker had always gotten a toy from those bags. I told him there was a toy but he would have to wait. Well, he didn't wait and while I was showing our guest to his room Tucker grew impatient and rummaged through the bags to find his toy. The food remained untouched but he was busily maiming the new toy when I returned.

His favorite toy was small and log shaped and he never maimed it or got sick of it. He would carry it around in his mouth and show it to everyone. It would often roll under a door or bookcase and he couldn't reach it. He would lie down and look at it out of his reach and fall asleep. If we saw him with his nose on the floor pointing under something we knew he was waiting patiently for someone to get his favorite toy back for him.

None of our previous pets would pee on command but Tucker would every time. Riding to Florida in the fall and back to Maine in the spring was a long way but no chore for any of us and particularly not for Tucker. He loved to ride, he loved to sit on a lap and look out the window, and although he was not one to snuggle he liked to be held while riding. We would ride for a few hours and stop at a rest area for a bathroom break for all of us. Tucker soon learned he couldn't do a lot of sniffing and socializing. If he forgot what he was supposed to do we would just say "GO PEE" and he would immediately. Although he was not housebroken when he arrived it didn't take long for him to learn.

He soon learned to kiss on command also. We would all sit around him on the bed and I would say, "Kiss Mom, Kiss Dad, Kiss Todd, Kiss…" whoever else was around that day. He would be correct nearly all the time and thought it was great fun. Of course he would always get a treat.

When he was six months old we took him to puppy obedience class. The instructor was pretty stuck on her theories and told me cockers could not easily be trained.

She had liver treats she had made that she swore every dog loves. Tucker didn't. She would teach us some of the things that Tucker had known forever like sit, stay, leave it, wait, heel, etc. She said several times that he probably wouldn't be able to do this or that. He had easily done everything she taught and she was soon using him to demonstrate to the other dogs how to do specific tricks. Since he didn't like the liver treats he did them without treats. She kept busy with the ill behaved so-called smart breeds and Tucker would start to doze from boredom. We didn't bother to go to all the classes.

When he was being groomed one time, his groomer grabbed her water bottle and took some gulps. He cocked his head and looked at me. I knew what he was thinking. We often gave him drinks out of his bottle on hot walks. I got his water bottle and he showed the groomer how he drank from a bottle just like she had done. She got quite a kick out of him.

Since this is a book of inn tales I should stick to the main theme and describe why Tucker was a great inn dog. First of all he loved children and would roll around the floor with them. He also would follow them when he could and try to do whatever they were doing. The only trouble arose when they came in through the door with a stuffed toy. He would try to grab it thinking it was a toy for him but after it happened the first time much to the child's chagrin I was poised to prevent it from happening again.

Some of our guests are children that come year after year. They remembered Tucker and would ask to play with him. I would show them his tricks and taught them how to do them. One of his favorites was the three cup magic trick. I would put a treat under one of the cups and he would wait and watch as I moved the cups around. I always left the treat in the middle cup so he knew right where it was. The kids were always impressed.

We have one room with a maid's entrance to our

private quarters. When it came time to do daily housekeeping we would leave the maid's entrance open. Tucker would often follow us in. This one time we spent a little longer because the TV remote needed reprogramming. We didn't pay much attention to Tucker and thought he must have gone back through the open door. About an hour later the guests returned to their room and were greeted by Tucker. They said he was awfully cute but they couldn't keep him. Didn't we want him back? He must have gone under the table with the long tablecloth and fallen asleep. We were so busy we hadn't missed him. Luckily the guests thought it was a hoot and told the story many times about Tucker surprising them in their room at Seacroft Inn.

Tucker didn't like it when people just appeared at the door without knocking or ringing the doorbell. He would sit at the bottom of the spiral staircase and give them warning barks until I came down the stairs. When he saw me he stopped his warning and immediately ran to greet them.

There was a time when I decided to clean the oven. It often would set the smoke alarms all blaring so I had waited until all the guests had gone for the day. I did not know the oven floor was covered with turkey juice. Not only were the alarms going off but the kitchen was full of acrid smoke. Tucker tried to get us out of the house. He kept running back and forth between the door and us. I saw Dave parked out front just returning from his job at the university. I always let Tucker out to greet him but instead of stopping where Dave was he kept on running out the drive. Dave said, "Where is he going?" He went after Tucker and brought him back. He had to pick Tucker up to get him back inside. Dave soon learned what was bothering him.

Tucker was unusually intelligent and sensitive to humans. He tried really hard to understand us when we talked to him. He would go eye to eye with us and cock his head. His big brown eyes were very expressive. I could tell most of the time what he was thinking. Dogs do not live long enough. They become close family members and are always there with you. When they are no longer a presence there is a huge void. It has been awhile since Tucker passed away. He was a wonderful pet, a beloved family member, and the perfect inn dog. We all miss him very much. My son Todd always called him Wonder Dog. I also think he was.

TABBIE IN THE CAT ROOM

It was autumn, the end of a busy tourist season, and the bridge ladies were meeting at Tabbie's home. The setting is gorgeous with public gardens all around and an 1880's quaint and quiet inn just across the street. There we can dine on the back deck that overlooks the harbor, still filled with private yachts and lobster boats. Meeting at Tabbie's elegant but comfortable home is always fun because we can always tour the gardens or lunch nearby on a lobster salad or seafood chowder before we shuffle the cards.

Tabbie has a great laugh and I hear it often while the eight of us are playing bridge. She is relating her summer story. Like so many of the inn and rental owners I know, Tabbie moves out of her home during the summer season and gets rewarded with healthy rental fees for the sacrifice. She started doing this years ago and thought it was profitable enough that she could have a nice apartment built over her garage. This would be the perfect place for her to live. It wasn't long before she realized she could rent the apartment out also. But where would she stay?

She hops among friends' homes, not staying too long in any one place so as not to wear out her welcome. When those possibilities run out, she moves into her son's home. He has no extra bedrooms but does have a small den with couch where she stays. She babysits and helps out where she can and makes do with the couch.

This past summer she realized that she had to share the den with their new family member, a cat named Fleas. Fleas quickly fell in love with her. The cat enjoyed sharing the couch with Tabbie and all night long would purr away to show its affection. Tabbie was relating this story to us as we played cards. Her signature laugh rang out as she said, " While complete strangers enjoy my nice roomy home, I have to sleep with Fleas."

IT SEEMS TO BE THE THING TO DO

So many if not all the inn owners that I know do the same thing that Tabbie does. They make the sacrifice of living outside their comfort zone to make the extra income. Some depend on it to pay their expenses. But others don't really need the money and are just being a bit greedy. I no doubt would have been just like them if Dave hadn't made sure we kept our inn small. He wanted it the size we could easily manage and our living space large enough to accommodate visiting family. My often-empty nest has 6 bedrooms and 4 baths. Our family knows they can come and go as they wish and there is always a place for them and their friends. We never felt uncomfortable in our home and always had plenty of room to move around. Maybe we could be considered space greedy.

Some inn and rental owners do strange things to make the extra income. One couple inherited a small inn right in the center of town. They lived in a basement apartment at the inn and made needed improvements in the 10 guest rooms. After the inn opened for the season, they started making small improvements in their apartment. They wanted it nice enough so they could rent it of course. As soon as they finished a home for them in the inn's back yard they rented out the basement apartment. While living in their home they started thinking about all the income their home could make if they rented it out for the tourist season. They still live there in the winter but bounce around summers finding room with relatives. They derive a very good income from a 10-room inn, a basement apartment, and a 3-bedroom home, but are pretty much homeless for 5 months a year. To them the extra income outweighs Comfort and Common Sense.

A single lady who for many years owned a large B&B in town made many improvements to the inside and outside of her property. She bought up land around it and eventually added on to it with the idea that she would make herself a nice space to live. She had been living in her basement for several years. Déjà vu all over again. She developed several nice suites and as you may have guessed used them as rentals. In the 40 years she ran that place she never moved out of the basement. Her guests had nicely appointed rooms or suites with balconies and she had cement walls and no windows. Living in the basement affected her health and she recently passed away.

The pattern continues with most lodging places in resort areas. Owners know there is good income in short term seasonal rentals so every space they can think of is turned into gold. Sacrifices are made and it seems okay with them because the money is good. So good that many of them have moved on and purchased other places of lodging. There are couples who now own several inns and yet they still sacrifice their comfort and sometimes health by living in tiny damp spaces. Is it really the right thing to do? Maybe for them but Not for me. I prefer to be Space Greedy.

BAR BAR BLACK SHEEP

The Porcupines are a group of islands that surround the town of Bar Harbor on two sides. You can guess why they are named after the prickly round backed little animals. They also have individual names that are sometimes difficult to remember. I devised a small verse taken from a famous nursery rhyme to teach my granddaughters the names.

Bar bar black Sheep Burnt his tail and before Long it was Bald! The islands are in a semi circle in this order, Bar, Sheep, Burnt, Long, and Bald. My granddaughters learned the island names quickly using this rhyme. A friend of mine, Polly, failed miserably. She gave up trying to learn the rhyme, so concentrated on just learning the names. She got most of them correct but the name of the last one did not come easily to her. She said, "Bar, Sheep, Burnt, Long, Crispy." We now often call Burnt Island, Crispy Island, in honor of Polly.

Polly is a skilled artist who lives in Brooklyn. She has shows in Manhattan, does Venetian plastering for famous celebrities, and is a master at matching colors. She is a friend who stays in my private tree house room on the third floor when she visits. Wanting to leave her mark on

Seacroft she spent hours painting a mural in that room. She used the linden tree just outside the window to inspire her and needless to say it is beautiful. Before she began I threatened to paint over it if I didn't like it but I would never really do that. The painting makes me feel like I am deep in a rain forest with the rich green colors.

I love Polly. Everyone is such a unique personality with his or her own skills and quirks. She may not remember the name of Burnt Island but she sure makes up for that with her kindness and being one of the most sincere human beings I know. It makes no difference to me or to anyone that Burnt Island has a new name, Crispy.

MOM MAKES FRIENDS WHEREVER SHE GOES

Todd says this phrase often, "Mom makes friends wherever she goes. "I sort of know what he means because sometimes I lack a filter and say what I am thinking. I asked him to give me some examples because I really couldn't think of too many incidents worthy of writing about. He emailed me the following stories and many I do not even remember. It is obvious to me that he embellished way too much and erased most of the reality of the situations. As I have mentioned before it is the Flavor and not the Facts that makes a story interesting. Todd has a great sense of humor and it is reflected in the emails he often writes to friends and relatives.

Some of these short stories have nothing to do with the inn, but my friend Polly, who read some of my inn stories, said I should write more about myself. She apparently thinks I am interesting enough to do this so with the help of Todd and the urging of Polly, here goes:

Hey, Mom,
I did a search of my "Sent Mail" and came up with the

following examples of you making friends wherever you go. They brought back some happy memories!!!

Email #1 The Much Coveted Munchkin

While we were in Ellsworth, Mom went into the new Dunkin' Donuts to get a couple sandwiches and some Munchkins for me. I requested jelly and chocolate-glazed which Mom ordered from the uninspired teen working behind the counter. He sleepily informed her that they were all out of jelly Munchkins, and they only had seven chocolate-glazed Munchkins left.

"Fine," Mom groused, "then just give me the seven chocolate Munchkins." It seemed to take forever to add up the order, collect Mom's money, and bag the coveted Munchkins. As he was doing this, another worker with a bitchy attitude breezed up behind him, snatched one of the chocolate Munchkins, and started to walk away. Teen boy said nothing but Mom bleated. "I already paid for that!" "I don't care," the worker replied, whirling around to face Mom. "Somebody else ordered it before you." Then she whirled around again and started to walk away when Mom snarled, "You bring back that Munchkin NOW!" in the tone of voice she sometimes uses to make a point. The worker wisely froze in mid-step, turned, brought the Munchkin back, dropped it in the bag, and then snootily said to Mom, "I'll just give him a whole donut," before walking away in a huff. "Good for you," Mom retorted. I've said it before and I'll say it again: Mom makes friends wherever she goes!

Email #2 Technologically Dependent

On Tuesday, I went to the podiatrist for a treatment on my painful foot. The treatment was incident-free, but Mom's paying for the appointment was a different story. All of the computers in the office were down, and the receptionist was practically useless.
MOM: I'd like to pay the bill with my credit card.

RECEPTIONIST: We'll run your credit card through, but it might not work.
MOM: Can you take cash?
RECEPTIONIST: Ummm...I don't know...
MOM: Do you need a computer to make change?
RECEPTIONIST: I guess not...
MOM: I'd like a receipt for that.
RECEPTIONIST: I can't print it off for you.
MOM: Do you have a pen and paper?
RECEPTIONIST: Yes...
MOM: Can't you write me out a receipt?
RECEPTIONIST: I guess so...
MOM (through gritted teeth): Thank you....

I've said it before and I'll say it again: Mom makes friends wherever she goes!

Email #3 Bunny, Be Nice!

Barb had a craving for seafood, so on Thursday we drove out to Pine Island and had lunch at a waterfront cafe, a funky eatery in St. James City. Situated on a canal, it has a back deck where we made ourselves comfortable and listened to the entertainment: a guitar-strumming hippie who warbled Jimmy Buffet songs and fought to stay vertical. Of course, Aunt Barb, who loves offbeat people and places, was right in her glory. Mom, on the other hand, wasn't quite as charmed.
Singer: I wrote this next song in honor of my first wife. We got divorced a month after I played it for her.
BARB: How many times have you been married?
Singer: Three!
MOM: You've got to stop writing songs.
Singer: (ignoring her): After my next song, I'll be taking a twenty-minute break.
MOM (under her breath): Don't feel you have to hurry.
Barb: Bunny, be nice!
Do you get the picture? I've said it before and I'll say it

again: Mom makes friends wherever she goes!

Email #4 Don't Trash Talk my Patriots

On Wednesday I had PT with Brad. The office was in a state of chaos because receptionist/major domo had fallen from a chair and broken her wrist in five places the night before so she was absent. Brad, one of the young PT Techs, was manning the office and I'm afraid Mom took him to the woodshed.

I overheard the following exchange from the reception area:

BRAD: (He knew I was a Patriot fan but he was soon to find out that Mom is also) Tom Brady really stunk up the joint during the Super Bowl, didn't he?

MOM: I thought he played really well. He gave the team an eight-point lead in the second half and kept his cool, even though his favorite target was gimpy and his left shoulder was injured.

BRAD: But he threw an interception! And some of his throws were way over the receivers' heads!

MOM: I suppose you could've done better.

BRAD: I would've rocked the joint!

MOM: Ya, right! You would have been creamed.

BRAD: I know. I was only kidding.

MOM: Let me guess, you're a Giants fan.

BRAD: Actually, I root for the Tampa Bay Buccaneers.

MOM (being sarcastic and laughing uncontrollably said): "Now, that's a good team." (At the time, it was one of the worst teams)

This exchange made me nervous since I depended on Brad to keep me upright while I was doing my physical therapy. I am happy to say he was professional and ignored Mom. He maintained a tight grip on my gait belt the whole time.

I've said it before and I'll say it again: Mom makes friends wherever she goes!

Email #5 The Standoff

In the late fall Mom went into The Guy Store to price some items she was considering giving for Christmas gifts, and she had the following exchange with the condescending store manager:

MOM: When are you going to have your end-of-the-season half price sale?

MAN (Indignant): Missy, I don't have to have a half-price sale. People buy my merchandise for full price or they don't buy it at all.

MOM (Bristling at being called "Missy"): All the storeowners I know tell me the tourists aren't buying much this year.

MAN: Well, you heard wrong, Missy. My store is wall-to-wall customers from the second I open to closing time.

MOM (Looking around the empty store): You certainly are busy now.

As you can imagine, Mom won't be buying anything from "The Guy Store" in the foreseeable future. I've said it before and I'll say it again:

Mom makes friends wherever she goes. (A little side note) That store is no longer in business.

The Filter Failed

This story is an inn story and I remember it well even though it happened at least three years ago. A couple came in to make a reservation for a specific room at a specific time one year from that day. Even though it was a long way off the room was already taken by a couple that reserved it every year. The man started whining and I thought he was going to cry. I told them I had the same room available at a different time and I had different rooms available for the same time if they could be flexible. The husband said they HAD to come at that time and they NEEDED that room because it had a full sized refrigerator for his beer. (All the other rooms have mini refrigerators). Oh Oh! I was thinking something, the filter came off, and I said it. "You sound just like a child." I haven't seen that couple since. I feel a little bad because I really liked the wife. She was standing behind him when I said what I said. She rolled her eyes at him and nodded yes to my comment. When I think of this incident I hear my son saying it again, "Mom makes friends wherever she goes!"

VISITORS OTHER THAN THE HUMAN KIND

Even though Seacroft is in town there is a variety of wildlife that wanders in from nearby woods and the National Park that is only a couple miles away. All year round deer can be seen on the Shore Path and on connecting streets. Every spring they meander up and down Albert Meadow, dine on my tulips, and then wander on to have dessert at my neighbor's garden on Elbow Lane. Later on in mid season after I have planted tomatoes and there are plenty of green ones, I notice that they immediately start disappearing. I can go from over 100 large green tomatoes to none overnight. My neighbor said the same thing. He has a fence around his but left the gate open one night and poof, the green tomatoes were gone.

Many of the locals do not like the deer for several reasons. I hear the complaints in stores and read about them in the paper. There is of course the loss of flower and vegetable gardens, the danger of Lyme Disease, and car/deer collisions. I love to have the deer and will happily feed them tulips and green tomatoes. Maybe it is to make up for the sadness I felt seeing the dead deer hanging off vehicles in hunting season or strung up in my childhood basement year round. Yes, Daddy was a poacher.

Another neighbor said he started to have mice in his house. With a Havahart Trap he collected 24 in a short while and deposited them several miles away. It was about the same time that I had evidence of a mouse on my bottom pantry shelf and in my snack drawer. I did not care to spare their little lives so used snap traps and cheese to get rid of a family of four. There is something about the wee creatures that just are not that endearing to me.

My whole family loves birds so we had lots of feeders on our deck. Unfortunately it became necessary to get rid of them because of all the issues they caused. There was a constant pile of seeds on the deck that led to one of our guest rooms. There seemed to be more pigeons and gray squirrels eating the seeds than the birds we intended to feed, the brightly colored ones we enjoyed watching up close. Where there is food, there is a variety of poop, running down the side of the inn and also coating the deck.

Dave used a Havahart Trap to catch squirrels. He would take them out into the park and release them. I could swear those same ones got back before he did. When he said he took them about 2 miles I told him they could cover that distance faster than he could even though he was a runner. The only way to correct this dirty situation was to take the feeders off the deck. It did get rid of the squirrels and pigeons, seed piles and poop, but it also got rid of the cardinals, sparrows, chickadees, grosbeaks, and other songbirds. It also brought a halt to our bird watching days.

I often see movement on the dimly lit deck at night through my patio door. It often is a family of raccoons looking for food or just out for a stroll. This is well and good as long as they don't frighten my guests who share the same deck. The raccoons often get on the guest room deck from the large cedar tree and amble down the stairs, across my deck, and out my front drive. So far no guests have met them face to face, at least that I know about.

Several years ago my neighbors allowed their two dogs to run loose. It is not really allowed in town and was not really appreciated by us the one time they spotted a small groundhog. Both dogs chased the little fellow under my deck. There were spits and squeaks from the groundhog and loud barking from the dogs. I knew that the guests would not appreciate the loud racket so close to their rooms. I asked the dog owners to come and get their dogs and solve the situation. The noise was not bothering them but they reluctantly climbed under the deck through the dirt and cobwebs to fetch their pesky pets. It took awhile before the two dusty neighbors emerged each grasping an agitated canine by the collar. A short while later I saw the little groundhog hightailing it out of my yard heading toward Elbow Lane where he could dine in peace.

Maine is famous for that clumsy big antlered animal, the moose. There are several stores in town with Moose in their names, The Black Moose, You and the Moose, Cool as a Moose, etc. This probably makes tourists think they might see one on the island at any moment. I am often asked where they might spot one. I have lived in Bar Harbor for 30 years and have seen one only once. Moose can swim to the island or walk across the bridge at night, but very few do. A moose sighting in the park or on the island is very rare. Often people do ask where they might travel to see one. The woods in western and northern Maine are loaded with them. I used to see them driving to work when I lived in the Western mountains. One thing that should be avoided at all cost is a car/moose collision. The moose generally wins. The passengers and driver are often seriously injured or killed.

Maine is a Wonderland of Wildlife of all kinds. It is one of the reasons I love the state so much. Seacroft is a great place for humans to stay while in Bar Harbor.

Apparently animals like it also. You might just see one on one of your stays.

When the worlds of humans and animals meet, the result is always interesting, sometimes funny, and never boring.

SEACROFT LAUNDRY SERVICE

There is a lot of laundry involved in the lodging business. The larger places send their laundry out to get washed and ironed. They are charged by the pound. Those thirsty towels can get pretty expensive to launder. Some places just send out their sheets and pillowcases and take care of the towels themselves. We tried sending our sheets out for a short while but it did not seem dependable. I only have two sets of sheets for each room and often I would not get them back on schedule. They would look very bright white and pressed but often smelled like smoke. The drivers of the delivery service were smokers and obviously smoked in their van. I quickly decided to keep laundering them myself.

At Seacroft we don't do daily maid service unless the guests request it and pay a little extra. It turns out that most guests prefer to take care of their rooms themselves if they have the choice. Saving a little money doesn't hurt either. If they want clean towels or linens they just have to place the used items outside their rooms before 10am and we replace everything they leave with fresh items. Sometimes there is a big heap and sometimes there is just one washcloth. More often than not there is nothing.

Some people are environmentally conscious and are careful not to put out the things they can reuse. Needless to say this lightens the laundry load.

When there is a big change over day there is a lot of laundry and several loads to do. I have two washers and two dryers. There is an average of at least four loads a day but often there could be eight or ten. This all has to be folded and the sheets and pillowcases need ironing. Kady seems to love ironing so she spends hours keeping up with that.

For years I had a clothesline and hung the sheets out. They smelled so fresh it changed the atmosphere of the whole room. Over the years this seemed to become too time consuming. The clothesline kept breaking over the winter when ice and snow fell from the high roof. Every spring it needed to be repaired. I finally decided to give up this process and had the decrepit lines taken down. I never have become sick of doing laundry. There is a great feeling to take the rumpled damp heaps and turn them into fresh and folded and organized piles for the shelf.

I have always offered a laundry service to my guests charging them $5 a load for a wash, dry, and fold. After having many extra large loads this past year I have decided to increase that to $10 a load. The bigger places charge that for laundering a shirt. Many guests prefer to do their own and would love to have me furnish a washer and dryer but I have no convenient place for that set up . We do have a Laundromat in town so if guests prefer, they can go that route. I do personal laundry after the inn laundry is out of the machines. I can often get their clean clothes back to them the same day. Many guests love this service as they much prefer to spend their time having fun rather than pacing in the Laundromat on a gorgeous sunny summer day.

There was a family that had three little boys all under the age of five. I have never seen so many little socks and whitie-tighties. It was years ago but I still remember how time consuming it was to match up those little socks and fold those little skivvies. That was a labor of love for me. I am sure the poor Mom did just that often and must have really appreciated my efforts.

A big catastrophe happened with one big load from an Australian couple. I was heading out for an errand to pick up supplies so was in a hurry. Kady was finishing up the rooms and laundry so I started the guest load. Being in a rush I added bleach to a colored load. I panicked and tried to undo my mistake but bleach acts fast and it is difficult with a front loader to stop the process. A long story short, I ruined practically all of this couple's travel clothes. I apologized profusely to them and offered to pay for the damages.

I couldn't have done this to a nicer party. They did not want any payment. They said unlike most travelers they preferred to travel with clothes that they soon planned to replace. They even threw out parts and pieces of their wardrobe as they approached the end of their travels preferring to make room in their bags for new purchases. What a relief! I could not have found a better situation for my huge error. I gave them a deal on their room even though they said it was not necessary. I still remember the gentleman laughing about the whole scene. In his adorable Australian accent he said he loved his new one of a kind tie-dyed knickers (boxers). He was going to keep those and show them to his friends back home. They were his Show and Tell to accompany his story of what happened to him while staying at Seacroft in Bar Harbor, Maine.

INNKEEPING 101

Tammy suggested this topic and title. She thinks I have come a long way in the business world for someone whose background was in education. I like to think that every career gets a little farther along with good common sense. Like most people I think I have pretty good common sense because I have created a successful business that I really enjoy. I have learned a lot along the way about the lodging business, about myself, and about people.

Starting a business from scratch is never easy but there are several common sense issues that I considered. The product and the location have to appeal to prospective customers. The energy of the business has to be positive and comfortable for owners, staff, and customers. The owners have to be acceptable to the amount of work it will take to not only get started but to persevere. The owners should enjoy every aspect of the business or at least most of them.

The owner should be a people person, or if not should work on the skills to become one of them. As in most situations "Patience is a Virtue." I have learned in most situations that "Honey will accomplish more than

Vinegar." In other words raising one's voice often does not get you very far. On the other hand one cannot assume that the "Customer is always Right" because very often he/she is not. The manager has to learn skills to handle difficult and demanding customers.

The product should be something that appeals to the masses. We started with the premise that if we liked something probably there are many others that would like the same thing. We wanted to keep our rates reasonable and in line with similar facilities, but at the same time we wanted to equip our rooms with everything that added to the guest's comfort and needs. At the beginning we did not want to deal with food or a.c.'s but discovered that we could increase our business if we did. We offered coffee right at the start, later added a breakfast option, and eventually and reluctantly added air conditioning.

We were not afraid to be a little different. Knowing people are always trying to save money we offered discounts at first for breakfast and housekeeping and later changed them to options at a reasonable add on rate. We witnessed that this made it more convenient for us and we are always looking for ways to save time as well as to save money for our guests. They would only pay for the extras they wanted. We also put mini kitchens in our rooms because that is what appealed to us and as it turned out it appealed to our guests. Also many customers have medicine that requires refrigeration. Seacroft Inn is often full and I get asked for recommendations for places like our inn. I can truthfully say there are none. Seacroft is unique in many aspects. Just a few are our quiet in town location, our low rates with options, and our mini kitchens. We also welcome children of all ages.

Our rooms are very homey like the traditional B&Bs but I know of no others that have in room refrigerators. I hear that more and more owners are now considering them, and I see them in hotel and motel rooms where they did not use to be. I remember being a child traveling with my family in the 50's. There were big signs in every motel room that read, "NO FOOD ALLOWED IN ROOMS." We had one big suitcase dedicated not only to food, but it also contained a coffee pot and toaster. We ate in the rooms in spite of the signs. We always tried not to make crumbs and we attempted to leave no trace of our transgression.

We do honor reasonable requests if a guest needs something, but we don't get a lot of them because our rooms are very well stocked with necessities. If there are enough requests for the same things such as wine glasses and wine bottle openers I just supply all the rooms with these popular items. Some requests such as ice for coolers get a polite refusal. Each room has a fridge with ice tray and we will supply enough ice for cocktails. However, we do not have the capacity to make a large supply of ice and are not big enough to install an icemaker.

Customers should be treated nicely and fairly because one should want them to be pleased enough to return. It is nice to see them back again the next year. I do not reserve more than a year in advance giving present guests the first chance to rent their room at the same time next year. Often guests become friends with other guests that always come at the same time. They sit on the lawn and catch up, hike together, or share a meal at a favorite restaurant. I often overhear them laughing as they share stories.

DIY projects are learned rapidly to save money. I often sew curtains and pillow covers, mend sheets and quilts, and fix toilets. Plumbing can be difficult but I have learned to shorten a chain with a safety pin, change a toilet handle, install a new flapper, and I am an expert plunger. Kady is an expert manning a toilet snake. I leave the tough stuff for the professionals. If I can't easily fix something I get on my phone for assistance. I am always careful to say if it is an emergency or not because if I do have an emergency I want them to respond quickly. I have had to call a plumber on Sunday because of no hot water and also one at two am for a bad toilet leak. Not a lot of serious off hours' emergencies for being in business for nearly thirty years.

Keeping things on the easy side is always on our minds. Many time consuming tasks are talked about and analyzed to see if we can come up with some ideas to simplify the situations. Hookless non-plastic shower curtains are wonderful, easily snapped on and off, and washable. I am not sure who invented them but that person must be very wealthy now. We keep supplies in several convenient spots to save time and energy. We only have white towels, facecloths, tub mats, sheets, and shower curtains. Whites can always be bleached and seem to last forever. Trying colors was unsuccessful because they quickly fade and look shabby. Color coding the rooms with different sheets and towels is classy but doesn't pass the Seacroft test of time. I have one repeat guest that put his foot through one of my older thinner sheets. He seemed quite perturbed at first but we simply made light of the situation and quickly changed his bed with a newer sheet. He then began to kid about it every year after that and said he was honored since he was sure George Washington must have slept in those sheets before him.

If someone asks me how he or she should start an inn business I would say, purchase your special place in a great location where people want to visit, create a place where you would love to stay, treat guests the way you would like to be treated, be willing to work hard but try to keep things simple, be willing to learn new skills, learn to love people from all backgrounds, be willing to offer a helping hand where needed, and while doing all this - HAVE FUN.

WHY I WEAR CLOTHES TO BED

This story is just one example of why I wear clothes to bed. Beatrice lives in an ocean resort town similar to Bar Harbor but she still comes to Seacroft about once a year if the weather permits. She watches the winds and the temperatures and will not come if everything is not perfect. In the middle of the night on one of her visits things did not go perfectly. She heard a gush of water and quickly called me. Luckily it was at the beginning of the season so I had a dry room vacant that I could move her into so she could hopefully get right back to sleep. I called the emergency number of the off hours plumber. As usual it would take about an hour for him to get there. Plumbers don't seem to live in Bar Harbor or even on the island.

I had trouble with the same leak the fall before so knew right where to look. The toilet shutoff in the room right over what was to be Beatrice' room was dripping steadily. Before I left Seacroft for the winter I had discovered a huge puddle where there hadn't been one the day before in the room where Beatrice would be staying. I called a plumber at that time to fix it. Instead of replacing the shut off he took a quarter turn with a great big wrench. It stopped the dripping so he said it was fine, and luckily it was fine all winter. In hindsight I wished he had replaced the shut off at that time rather than wield the huge wrench.

When I turned the toilet back on that next spring it began to drip and accumulate enough to run into the room below - Beatrice's room. I was not aware that this was happening until I got Beatrice's call in the middle of the night. Putting towels down absorbed most of the water until the plumber arrived. I had told him to make sure he had a new shutoff part with him and he did. At 2 AM I sat on the edge of the tub in Room 3 chatting with Charlie as he replaced the part. I really can't remember what we talked about but he suggested I just leave the toilets turned on over the winter since the shutoffs do wear out after awhile if turned off and on enough times.

I was dressed in my usual night clothes that were really loose fitting day clothes. Even before we owned the inn I was not comfortable in anything flimsy at night. With the children so small at one time, then the older children, then the inn guests, I wanted to be properly covered so I could react quickly if there were an emergency. That is why I wear clothes to bed. Like the boy scouts, I want to Be Prepared.

The shutoff was soon replaced and the leak was fixed. Clean up in the room below could wait until morning. Charlie went home an hour away and I went back to bed with my clothes on.

I saw Beatrice the next day and apologized for the inconvenience. I also refunded her money for both nights. She thought I should only refund one night but I insisted on the two night refund. The next morning she checked out and left a nice note. She said the plumber would charge me for overtime. Beside the note was a crisp fifty dollar bill.

PET PEEVES

Everyone has pet peeves. Some show a bit more disgust than others. I might be one of them. I have listed a few that quickly come to mind, and I have categorized them into three sections.

Those Pet Peeves That Need No Explanation

A few pet peeves I possess are late night arrivals, late night phone calls, late night flushes (do you see a pattern here?), stained tub mats, seal, and grout, peeling wallpaper, carpet and laundry stains that refuse to come out no matter what, furnace malfunction in the winter, frozen pipes, cigarette butts, litter, telemarketers - especially the recorded kind because you can't complain to them, plaster cracks, and repairmen that don't succeed.

Those Pet Peeves That I Have Already Mentioned

I did mention insensitive smokers, crazy people at weddings, overuse of air conditioning, stuffy rooms, baking, breakfast baskets, false smoke alarms, guests that don't respond to the sound of blaring alarms, too many cruise ships at the same time, difficult guests, and hairs, hairs, everywhere.

Those Pet Peeves That Might Need Some Explanations With Examples From the Inn

One example would be guests that say they are bored and often ask me what they should do because in their minds they have seen everything. They have been in town for one full day, have walked around the shops, dined in two different restaurants, and had an ice cream cone. I ask, "Have you strolled on the Shore Path?" "No!" "Have you been in Acadia yet?" "No!" "Have you taken a hike?" "No!" "Have you taken a boat trip?" "No!" "Have you biked on the Carriage Roads?" "No!" "Have you been to the other towns on the island?" "No!" "Have you been to one of our museums?" "No" "Have you been to Wildwood Stables and lined up a carriage ride?" "No!" "Are you interested in rock climbing, stand up paddle boating, or ghost tours?" "No!" "Do any of these things appeal to you?" If the answer is still a big fat "No!" then they are vacationing in the wrong place. It is a huge pet peeve when I hear "We have seen everything," and they just arrived that day. It happens.

Loud noises bother me. Leaf blowers are extremely loud and are used often in my neighborhood. Early morning mowing and construction banging are irritants to guests that want to sleep a little later. Inebriated neighbors that play with lighted Frisbees in the middle of the night are a bother when they awaken guests. Loud tv's, loud voices, loud steps on the stairs are also pet peeves of mine. I just do not like LOUD anything.

When groups reserve rooms at the inn I have to cringe a little for several reasons. They come at the same time and leave at the same time. When this happens there is a lot of cleaning and laundry on the arrival as well as the departure day. Groups can block up time frames preventing a more staggered pattern that is easier on the staff, (Kady and me). Members of a group tend to hang around and socialize with each other rather than take off for the day to enjoy the park. Before the arrival date if one person in the group dies, gets ill or injured, or has an important function that arises such as a wedding, the whole group often cancels. I have saved several rooms for several days turning down many others that would have come. During the year reservations come filtering in and fit together like pieces of a puzzle. When cancellations occur it is like a puzzle that becomes ruined when some of its pieces go missing. There are a bunch of holes.

Annoying scents such as peppery perfumes, men's colognes, cigars, burned popcorn, and dirty diapers are troublesome. Sometimes it takes days to rid the rooms of these assorted scents. Some people are more sensitive to smells than others. Some ladies apply perfume in excess because to them it takes a lot to get the desired effect. It can be overpowering to others. Men's cologne usually stays in a room longer then perfume no matter what we do. Airplanes have a "Please No Perfumes Policy" for the comfort of others in the small space. I would like to do the same at the inn.

We have nice black facecloths at Seacroft that are monogrammed MAKEUP. They are placed right beside the sink along with the white facecloths. It is disheartening when they remain unused and the expensive white facecloths have to be relegated to the rag pile because they are ruined beyond repair.

A big pet peeve is that guests often don't read the information on their room door. They will be here for days but will ask me all the questions that are covered on the information sheet. Where is the trash container, do you recycle, what do I do with the towels, do you have umbrellas, when is check out time??????? I even leave small notes by their room keys that state, "We are a unique inn and do some things differently. Please take a minute to check the information by your door."

I used to have a small sign by the doorbell that said, "Always ring doorbell, then enter." Most guests not only ignored the sign but also came in through two doors as quietly as they could and I had no idea they have arrived. They still do this, and they probably always will. They stand at the desk wondering why I am not there. I now have a second doorbell on the inside door but most also walk right by that without using it. I have learned that if I am not in the immediate vicinity of the front desk I need to lock the inside door. Then and only then will I hear the doorbell ring.

Making a bed with a bed ruffle is a definite pet peeve. Once I mistakenly purchased queen comforters for my queen beds. I know this makes sense but queen comforters require that you have a bed ruffle to cover the box spring. I usually purchase king sized quilts that are large enough to cover the bottom of the bed so I can dispense with the ruffle. It is much more difficult to make a bed with a dust ruffle because it takes three hands. That third hand is helpful to hold the ruffle down while you tuck in the bedding with the other two hands. It is possible to make a bed with two hands but it is a time consuming hassle. I now remember the extra time it takes to make a bed with a ruffle and on the next orders I will surely get the quilts king sized.

I dare say that blackout curtains can be found in every place of lodging except Seacroft. I find a lot of broken gear on heavy curtains in the places I stay. I don't like things that don't work well so chose not to install all the paraphernalia needed to pull heavy drapes across the windows and back again. I make privacy curtains from translucent white or off white material that can be pulled back and forth easily with rings on a rod. The rooms stay light and airy. Some people complain that with the sun rising early they are awakened before they are ready to start their day. There is no sympathy from me. I think my guests should get up and get going early. It is a great time to walk the Shore Path or on Sand Beach in Acadia. There are very few others out and about early. If guests complain about the park being too busy I tell them to get up with the sun. That would be around 5 AM. They will find the whole park easily accessible and pretty much to themselves. Some of them actually thank me for the suggestion.

When August arrives it is officially the middle of the peak tourist season. Often there are three cruise ships anchored in the harbor. Tourists have arrived in huge numbers trying to enjoy their last chance for a summer vacation. By then owners, managers, and employees in our stores and places of lodging are getting worn down from dealing with hoards of humans. If you are visiting Bar Harbor at that time you might witness a bit of what we call August Attitude. It hopefully improves as tourism lets up somewhat by the end of the month. Autumn is just around the corner and the end of another season is in sight. Smiles return and attitudes cool off along with the fall weather. It is time for this Bar Harbor inn owner to start doing fall chores and planning for the trip south.

In reading this story over it sounds as if I am a very negative person. As Kady says, my August Attitude starts really early - the first of May. I have learned for the most part to smile and handle situations professionally. I am thankful for my guests that are wonderful people and do not cause any serious issues. Bar Harbor is a great place to live and work. Opportunity Abounds and Life is Good. I guess I will be a little more positive and instead of calling the above subjects, pet peeves, I will just call them minor annoyances. Minor annoyances can be easily handled.

THE PROS AND CONS OF A HOME AND BUSINESS COMBINATION

I like it a lot, some days more than others. As with practically everything there are some Cons. The owner may feel comfortably at home with no cares, but he or she is always aware that any minute a guest might need something, ask directions, or cause an issue. I am technically available twenty-four hours a day but guests generally take care of themselves and don't want to disturb me. There might be a request for clean linens because three-year-old Leno wet the bed. Joe might come to the office for some ice because he wants to make cocktails for him and his wife. There might be a bad leak in one of the rooms in the middle of the night. A plumber has to be called and the guest has to be relocated to a dry and comfortable place.

What do I do when the very loud and very alarming smoke detectors decide to go off for no reason? Regulations require them to be hardwired that simply means if one goes off they all go off in every guest room as well as in our private quarters. I have to walk around the inn inside and out to see if I can detect any smoke or reason for the alarm to sound. It is interesting to note that absolutely no guests come out of their rooms. If it is the middle of the night they do not even turn on their lights. I realized after a false alarm that if there really were a fire or dangerous situation I would have to pound on every door and make certain everyone gets outside. I often go through evacuation plans in my head with different scenarios.

Cons also include some really busy times that I am running ragged but those are few and far between. I cannot say, "There is Never a Dull Moment," because there are many quiet times. One Con that cannot really be controlled is a high number of check outs and check ins on the same day. This often happens with groups such as weddings or with several couples traveling together. This always means a lot of cleaning and a lot of laundry and a lot of time. If several parties leave late it shortens the time we have to turn rooms around. A morning like this might be described as having "Never a Dull Moment." Usually however by noontime things are under control. All the check outs have left the grounds and most of the rooms are readied for the next round of guests. I must say when this happens it is very satisfying. The main activity for the afternoon is leisurely checking in guests, folding and ironing laundry, and catching some quiet moments on the couch.

The Pros of a combined home and business are many and probably obvious. The money is very good and because of the way the inn is run I am able to do it long after most people retire. I enjoy meeting interesting people from all over the world. I also enjoy reuniting with repeat customers that come every year, mostly from New England and the East Coast.

Being at home means I may have friends and family visit and still run my business. They often pitch in and help. If I am out I can always put notes on the door giving directions to rooms. If I am in the shower or off on an errand I can put my plastic clock on the door with a return time. I can put coffee out in the morning and take off for a two mile walk. Usually I am back before anyone is even up. I can play Bridge with the ladies and check people in if they come during the game. The ladies are all retired or semi retired and they know that my home is also my business. They just continue to socialize until I am finished.

I can deal with outdoor details like collecting trash, sorting recyclables, watering and deadheading plants, or wiping dew off the patio furniture. It is actually a great time to talk with guests when they come and go.

I love my home and its wonderful location. I love my business and love that my guests, my family, and my friends like to visit. I might have an occasional bad day when several things go awry, but they are few and far between. The Pros far outweigh the Cons just like my good guests far outweigh the bad. Because I work only six months of the year and completely get away from the business for six months in the winter I have created an excellent balance. I am always looking forward to the next move, to the warmer Florida climate winters and to the more comfortable Maine climate summers. Often guests say it sounds like a great life. They never say I am lucky because they know that it took a lot of hard work on my part to accomplish what I have achieved.

THEN AND NOW

In the past thirty years Bar Harbor has changed, Seacroft Inn has changed, and I have changed. Thirty years sounds like a long time but it has zipped by rapidly. When we first moved back in the early nineties, Bar Harbor was a small town and had that small town flavor. Winters were very cold, dark, and damp with countless short sunless days. Most of the shops and restaurants were closed. The streets were gray and quiet. Snow came early, usually toward the end of October. We would watch the last of the autumn leaves fall to the ground along with the snowflakes. Across Albert Meadow the rock maples kept their leaves tightly attached a bit longer and the bright red foliage would contrast with the new white snow

I am not a winter person, never liking to feel cold, so it was a time for me to crank up the heat and sit by the fireplace. I have a few really nice memories of family gatherings and twinkling Christmas trees in the sunroom. There were a few sunny days when we would don our x-c skis and slide around the Carriage Roads never seeing another human. There was that occasional day when the weather was just right and we would climb Cadillac Mountain on skis. The iced branches over our heads would glisten with the bright sunshine. We would get some nice snow, sometimes a lot of that white stuff. It would be perfect for winter sports, but – all too soon it would rain or melt and then freeze into a skating rink on steps and driveways. I would feel depressed with the darkness, biting cold, and having to be inside too long. I talk of Maine winters as if they were in the past because I am no longer there during that season.

I began to dream of spending winters in Florida where we could wear shorts and go barefoot and the sun would shine all day long. After years of paying off college bills for our kids and the mortgage on Seacroft we built a small home in a great family neighborhood in Cape Coral, nearly 1800 miles from Maine. We now look forward to heading south in October when the inn business is declining and the weather is getting colder.

We have watched Bar Harbor change over the years. It still manages to keep its 5,000 residents winters but balloons to millions during the summer season. Most of the few small motels built in the 50's still hang on today. They replaced the large hotels built in the 1800's to house the many rusticators that began visiting the island summers. Now large two hundred bed hotels have made a comeback and can be seen on every corner. Many visitors prefer the smaller inns and B&B's hanging onto the small town flavor they remember. July and August used to be the busiest months, but now our tourist season is a bustling six months long. We have hit a point of crisis where it is difficult to drive in Acadia and walk down the sidewalks of town because of so many visitors.

There are more and more shops and eateries every year. Some enterprising folks try to come up with a new twist in a business but the old favorites survive while the new ones often flop. A pizza place replaced a Greek restaurant, an ice cream shop replaced a specialty shop call Bra Harbor (it was worth a try but didn't make it), coffee and pastry shops are popular, and tee shirt shops outnumber them all.

There are many places to eat in town, all within walking distance from Seacroft, but the favorite place is any place that serves a good Maine lobster. That will never change.

Payphones have been replaced by cell phones. Many a person walks down the sidewalk with a phone glued to the nose. Free WiFi is offered in every park, coffee shop, and lodging facility. The ferry service between Canada and Bar Harbor has long disappeared and we now have Cruise ships anchoring almost daily, sometimes more than one a day. Fishing and lobstering while once were the biggest industries have been replaced at the top by tourism. Private yachts and schooners are anchored in the harbor outnumbering the working vessels.

Seacroft Inn has gone through many changes. There are major fixes and small improvements every year. Our ocean view has pretty much disappeared with neighbors raising their roofs and tree growth. The dreaded basement washers and dryers have been moved to a convenient location on the first floor. Shelves have been built in every corner for storage of linens, towels, comforters, and assorted inn supplies. Rates have gone up but still remain much lower than those of fellow inns. The phone used to ring off the hook and it was difficult to get much done. It hardly rings now because many guests prefer registering on our website. It is much more peaceful and less time consuming which is appreciated.

I have changed, too. Of course I am thirty years older than when we first started this business. I have learned the lodging business first hand and still enjoy it immensely. There is a lot less energy in this old girl now. When we were first open and Dave was at the university, I would clean all the rooms, run up and down the cellar stairs doing laundry, complete other assorted jobs, and put notes on the door for incoming guests so they could find their rooms. I would sneak away and bike the five miles to the top of the mountain (all up hill) and back again (all downhill) to be on hand for phone calls and guests that needed assistance. Now I leave the biking to the younger crowd and I take afternoon naps.

The future is a mystery. Who really knows about tomorrow? I believe one thing will never change. Folks from all over the world will still visit Acadia National Park and Bar Harbor. I know also that the great guests will always outnumber the questionable characters. Seacroft will be here for as long as I am here. Now that I am in my 70's guests who have been coming for years look at my wrinkles and ask how long I will keep Seacroft. With Kady's help I hope to be here for a long time. I have come up with some unique tactics that make the inn business easier for us to manage. As long as my guests are happy and keep coming back I will happily keep chugging along with a smile on my face. Kady says I have August Attitude that starts the first of May. I say she is obnoxiously positive, so I believe we complement each other. She is definitely more patient than me with difficult guests so I always get her to deal with them. Luckily for us there are very few of them. I am proud to say that Seacroft Inn is a success.

I am not only proud of Seacroft , I am proud of myself for creating something so special. Thank you, all, who have come to check us out. An enormous thank you to all that return year after year. There are so many that I didn't mention, G&G, J&J, B&C, F&M, S,L&J, K&B, J&P, J&K, D,J,&J, R&M, etc. You came as a guest, so many of you return as a friend.

ABOUT THE AUTHOR

Bunny Brown lives with her son at Seacroft Inn in Bar Harbor, Maine enjoying the busy summers and fall colors, while they spend winters in Cape Coral, Florida. Upon graduation from Springfield College in 1964 she and her husband Dave lived in Bar Harbor for three years which gave them an appreciation for the small Maine town. They left in 1967, but returned in 1990 to start their non-traditional inn. The coastal location adjacent to Acadia National Park allowed many opportunities for biking, hiking, kayaking, and cross-country skiing when not engaged with their guests. Bunny also enjoys spending time with her two daughters and her two granddaughters.

28042090R00087

Made in the USA
Columbia, SC
05 October 2018